THE POETRY
BUSINESS

THE POETRY BUSINESS

Peter Finch

seren

seren is the imprint of
Poetry Wales Press Ltd
Wyndham Street, Bridgend
Mid Glamorgan, Wales

A British Library Cataloguing in Publication Record
is available at the CIP Office

ISBN 1-85411-107-8

*The publisher acknowledges the financial support of the
Arts Council of Wales*

Printed in Palatino by WBC Bookbinders, Bridgend

Contents

	Introduction	7
1.	Where It All Begins: Sending In Your Stuff	9
2.	Competitions	16
3.	The Reading	23
4.	Groups of Poets: Circles, Classes, Courses and Societies for the Writer	30
5.	Bringing Out Your First Book	38
6.	Why Do You Publish — Ego Or Art? The Vanity Press	47
7.	Doing It Yourself	53
8.	The Literary Magazine — A Round-Up Of The Main Operators	60
9.	Specialist Poetry Mags: Clans, Denominations and Cabals	67
10.	The Little Littles: The Small Magazines	74
11.	The Book In Hand: Commercial and Specialist Publishers	80
12.	Small Presses: The Final Frontier	91
Appendix I:	Books for the Poet	102
Appendix II:	Bookshops	107
Appendix III:	Some Poetry Competitions	109
Appendix IV:	Writers' Groups Meeting in Wales	115
Appendix V:	Poetry Small Mags: Addresses	122
Appendix VI:	Poetry Small Presses: Addresses	127

Introduction

The Poetry Business began as a series of articles commissioned by the editor of *Poetry Wales*, Mike Jenkins. Mike wanted to round out his magazine of verse and criticism with an introduction to the workings of the poetry scene to be aimed as much at the hardened literateur as the stumbling beginner. To the outsider the business of poetry appears either transparently simple or impossibly complex. What I wanted to show was the middle path. In revising the material to make a book I have been strongly aware of the impermanence of almost everything. In the short period between completing the chapters and now, commercial publishers have changed their allegiances, organisations have closed down, and magazines have moved their addresses like travellers. At the time of writing things are correct again, at least as much as I can make them, but I can't see them staying that way.

The business aspect to all this is really a misnomer. No one makes any money from poetry except maybe those one or two at the very top — Ted Hughes, Seamus Heaney — or those who work as performers — Roger McGough, Benjamin Zephaniah. For most of us it is a suffering of what Roger Caldwell calls "the feeling of guilt at doing something so unprofitable, little-esteemed and to all outward appearances joyless as writing poetry; an activity which demands time out from daily responsibilities, from family and friends, time which has often to be fabricated at some cost". Yet we persist. Naturally enough there is a Welsh angle to some of the information I have compiled but never so dominant as to prevent the book being of use to poets everywhere. Indeed there is as much in here for verse writers in Caithness as there is for poets in Cardiff. Check it out. If there are gaps then please let me know. Write to me care of Seren.

In Hull Peter Sansom and Janet Fisher have for some years been running an excellent information, criticism and publishing operation also called The Poetry Business. There is no connection between us but as I have appropriated their name for this present work I dedicate it to them. Peter's own book, *Writing Poems*, comes from Bloodaxe. It's worth a read.

Peter Finch

Chapter One

Where It All Begins:
Sending In Your Stuff

I used to think that everyone did this all the time. In my days as a magazine editor it seemed that half of Wales and their uncle were determined to get themselves published and my magazine was the chosen place. Floods of poetry, all shapes, all sizes, arrived by all mails. I made the mistake once of going away on holiday unannounced and when I got back couldn't open the front door for the stack of unsolicited offerings piled up in the hall.

Anglo-Welsh poets used a variety of approaches. The late John Tripp would pass me his badly typed scripts in the pub. The ribbon on his machine was permanently out of alignment which resulted in everything coming out half black and half red. I'd find them in my back pocket the following day and wonder how they got there. Tom Earley's secretary-prepared golf-ball jobs arrived in large, flat envelopes by first class post, while Tony Curtis' mss would be accompanied by letters asking if, on acceptance, he would be entitled to two copies of the issue concerned since he would then be both a subscriber and a contributor. Most material, however, reached me in awful condition.

There would be illegible, hand-written poems on scrappy Woolworth's notepads; minimalist verse from America with no return postage; five thousand line epics bound up in hard-backed files which omitted all reference to who the author might be; great wodges of triple-spaced text with each page individually folded, paper-clipped and strung so securely that I'd need a pair of scissors and a spare half-hour just to open them; poetry illustrated by photographs of the landscape which inspired it or, worse, by close-ups of the person who wrote it; material accompanied by lengthy amplification, justification and description, endless detail of the author's military service and achievements in the fields of hang-gliding and cactus recognition with appended perhaps the kind words made in an unguarded moment by worthies such as Harry Secombe, Sir Edmund Hilary or the Aga Khan; poems fixed into lever-arch files and delivered by Securicor; poems accompanied by persuasive argument, by pleas for help, by threats, by bribes; occasionally poems accompanied by jolly authors in person hiccupping and slurring; work read down the telephone at 3 am because that was when the inspiration was hot; poems delivered by friends who would all want to wait for an immediate answer; unreadable stuff done with John Bull printing outfits; blurred photocopies; faded carbons; poems copiously illustrated, once pasted into the centre of an oil painted seascape but more often surrounded by squiggles and doodles left there no doubt as evidence of the virility of the author's muse. All of this was often just too much. We editors are unpaid activists running magazines in our spare time. How are we supposed to cope?

There are some around, of course, who get along by not actually reading anything at all. You can tell this by the massive unevenness of their periodicals. Their approach is usually along the lines of 'ah Minhinnick — I've heard of him — I'll use the lot'. Others employ whole teams of sub-editors in order to give every submission at least a complete read (as *Envoi* did when Anne Lewis Smith was editor in west Wales) and sadly end up excluding anything which is even slightly individual. Most, however, compromise and read only the first page of any batch of poems or sometimes even only the first few lines. How else do you manage to get through upwards of 20,000 hopeful bits of verse a year? And believe me, for a successful magazine that figure is not untypical.

Is there no respite? Apparently not. Things are due to get worse. Poets are on the increase. Creative writing classes are booming. Poetry is looking for a public, and the personal notebook is no longer enough. For those of you on the verge of sending off, what advice can I offer? If I was still editing I might suggest that you keep your head down for a few years until the verbal dust settles and you are more sure of what you are doing. There is nothing worse than having sloppy juvenilia around to haunt your more mature work later on. But most of you are no doubt at your peak producing poetry of the 90s and unable to wait. Obviously now is the time.

The best approach is to find ways of increasing your chances of getting your material accepted. There are literally thousands of people writing poetry, probably more now than at any other single time in history. Competition is intense but there are opportunities around. Forget about *The Independent's* daily poem, the Sunday papers, the *TLS* and those poems you see enshrined in places like

New Statesman and Society and *The London Review of Books*. These are difficult, competitive arenas. The big market for the new poet is the little magazine.

Such periodicals usually get published not because there is a particular need for them in the way that, say, the huge DIY industry needs a magazine for its customers, or that the growth of interest in computers has led to a range of dedicated home micro mags. New little magazines do not start because large numbers of readers suddenly want to spend more of their time consuming new verse or avant garde fiction. Purely from the reader's point of view there are too many anyway. Who could possibly get through 300 literary mags a year?

Most magazines actually begin not because of the readers but because of the writers. Maybe the editor has an interest in a particular type of poetry or in work from a specific geographical area or perhaps it is more a matter of getting him or herself into print and starting up a mag has been selected as the way. Circulations are painfully small and initially readers are almost always the writers themselves. In fact with a number of highly esoteric operations I wonder if there are any real *readers*. Certainly, to judge from what gets printed in a few places, the editors haven't bothered. Many literary magazines outgrow this stage, of course. As they go on they gain confidence, and they gain reputation. Yet despite this their overall sales still remain low.

The first certainty of the poetry business is that if your work is anything like even vaguely competent then you will find publication. As I've suggested you'll also have a pretty good chance if you write rubbish. There can be a lot of luck in this game. Do remember, though, that all publication is not equal. Getting a poem into *Planet* or *Stand* is relatively hard. They don't publish that many, they pay so competition is high, and they are critical — in the literary sense — about what they use. Not so with the likes of the *Hip Hop Gazette*. Here most things are welcome, contributions are scarce; almost anything goes. The magazine is the editor's hobby, like CB radio or train spotting, and has that intensity and flavour. But it is a place to start.

So what do you do to increase your chances?

* Follow the standard rules of manuscript presentation and submission. Everything typed, single side of A4 paper, one poem per sheet, titles and your name and address on everything. Keep a copy. Keep a record of what you send where and when. Submit half a dozen poems a time with a short covering letter saying who you are and, vitally important, enclose a suitably sized stamped addressed envelope for the reply.

* Read as much as you can so that you get to know what is fashionable, what is currently regarded as good, who is writing what and how. This way you will improve your own critical faculty and thereby raise standards. Buying a few small mags will help the editor's belief in what they are doing as well.

* Keep your ear to the ground to find out what small magazines are around. Most carry brief listings of others similar to themselves. Read Chapters Eight, Nine and Ten which survey the scene. Check the following specialist directories which give more comprehensive coverage. Send off for the smaller ones, consult the biggies at the library.

Small Presses of the UK & Ireland — An Address List (eleventh edition 1994 with hundreds of addresses) — published jointly by Oriel Bookshop (The Friary, Cardiff, CF1 4AA) and the Association of Little Presses.

The Writer's Handbook (annual) — edited by Barry Turner for Macmillan.

Light's List of Literary Magazines (200 UK addresses) — John Light, The Lighthouse, 29 Longfield Road, Tring, Herts., HP23 4DG.

Poet's Market (a massive American directory) — Writer's Digest Books, 1507 Dana Avenue, Cincinnati, Ohio 45207, USA.

Poetry Magazines (a current awareness list) — available in exchange for one SAE from the Poetry Library, Royal Festival Hall, Southbank Centre, London, SE1 8XX.

Directory of Poetry Publishers edited by Len Fulton (the original source for poetry addresses worldwide) Dustbooks, PO Box 100, Paradise, California 95969, USA.

WHERE IT ALL BEGINS

Poetry Ireland News Magazines List — 44 Upper Mount Street, Dublin 2.

Eastpress (small presses and little mags in Bedfordshire, Essex, Cambridgeshire, Hertfordshire, Lincolnshire, Norfolk and Suffolk) — Compiled by Eric Ratcliffe at Ore, 7 The Towers, Stevenage, Herts., SG1 1HE.

Magazines and Literary Journals: A Guide (list of main outlets plus descriptions) — compiled by Mark Robinson, Cleveland Arts, 7-9 Eastbourne Road, Linthorpe, Middlesborough TS5 6QS.

British Literary Periodicals (a selected bibliography of everything literary) — The British Council, 10 Spring Gardens, London, SW1A 2BN.

The Salmon Guide To Poetry Publishing In Ireland (lists magazines, newspapers and book publishers) — Salmon Publishing, Auburn, Upper Fairhill, Galway, Eire.

Quite a number of well known poets never send their material out speculatively at all. Ifor Thomas reckons that it is the performance of the poem that is important and not its printed publication, Tom Raworth has only ever responded to direct requests to him for material, while Dannie Abse hardly needs to send anywhere. Demand outstrips supply. It is the postion we would all like to be in. But the groundwork of getting yourself known has to be done at some stage. Be patient, be determined. Don't send blindly, read the magazine first. Be as professional as you can. Remember that even R.S. Thomas had a hard time of it when he started out. If you live in Wales you might like to try a few of these magazines all of which publish some poetry:

Borderlines, Journal of the Anglo-Welsh Poetry Society, Robin ap Cynon and Dave Bingham, 20 Hodgebower, Ironbridge, Shropshire, TF8 7QC. (Poetry small mag.)

BWA, Bulletin of the Welsh Academy, Third Floor, Mount Stuart House, Mount Stuart Square, Cardiff, CF1 6DQ. (Mainly news and reviews but does include the occasional pertinent poem.)

The Cardiff Poet, Eugene Nowakowski, 123 Coedpenmaen Road, Pontypridd, Mid Glamorgan, CF37 4LH. (Little magazine of the Capital's verse. *Valleys Poet* published by the same editor.)

Direction Poetry, P. Harrison, 28 Nant-y-Felin, Pentraeth, Anglesey, Gwynedd, LL75 8UY. (Verse on cassette.)

Fire, Chris Ozzard & Jeremy Hilton, 1 Gwar Gate, Cwmann, Lampeter, Dyfed, SA48 8JP. (Journal of new poetries.)

Grey Suit, Anthony Howell & Anna Petrie, 21 Augusta Street, Adamsdown, Cardiff, CF2 1EN. (Professionally produced video arts magazine which includes readings and performances by 'key poets'.)

Hrafnhoh, Joseph Buddulph, 32 Stryd Ebeneser, Pontypridd, Mid Glamorgan, CF37 5PB. (Self styled 'magazine for fuddy-duddies and lovers of eld', mainly family history and notes on little used languages but includes some verse.)

Making Waves, Jackie Aplin, Coptic House, 4-5 Mount Stuart Square, Cardiff, CF1 6EE. (Monthly Cardiff news and community magazine which always includes some local verse.)

New Lines, Joe Kelly, P.O. Box 658, Mold, Clwyd, CH7 lFB. (4 page monthly tabloid review of writing and writers in North Wales. Open to verse contributions from North Wales based poets.)

Merlin, Eurwen Price, Y Garn, Swansea Road, Llewitha, Fforestfach, Swansea, SA5 4NR. (Occasional journal of the West Wales writers' groups. Includes some poetry.)

New Welsh Review, Robin Reeves, room 1-8, 49 Park Place, Cardiff, CF19 3AY. (Professional journal of poetry, prose and criticism. Pays contributors.)

Paladin, Ken Morgan, 66 Heywood Court, Tenby, Dyfed, SA70 8DE. (Occasional, privately run small mag.)

The Pen Magazine, Pam Probert, 15 Berwyn Place, Penlan, Swansea, W. Glamorgan, SA5 7AX. (Aspiring writers' journal including both short fiction and poetry.)

Planet, John Barnie, P.O. Box 44, Aberystwyth, Dyfed. (The Welsh Internationalist. Professional cultural journal which uses poetry every issue.)

Poetry Wales, Richard Poole, Glan-y-Werydd, Llandanwg, Harlech, Gwynedd, LL46 2SD. (Mainstay of the poetry scene in Wales. Professionally published by Seren).

Red Poets' Society, Mike Jenkins, 26 St Andrews Close, Heolgerrig, Merthyr Tydfil, Mid Glamorgan, CF48 1SS. (Occasional collections of Welsh-based socialist verse published in association with *Y Faner Goch*.)

Spear, Jacqueline Jones, 2 Fforest Rd, Lampeter, Dyfed. (Small mag featuring science fiction, cartoon strips and poetry.)

WHERE IT ALL BEGINS

SWAG, c/o Jen Wilson, 8 Chaddesley Terrace, Swansea. (Magazine of the Swansea Writers' & Artists' Group but open to all.)

Swansea Arts Magazine, Tess Moran, c/o Students Union, University College Swansea, Singleton Park, Swansea, SA2 8PP. (Collectively run what's on around Swansea including at least four pages of poetry. Contributions from outside the University welcome.)

Swansea Review, Glyn Pursglove, Dept. of English, University College Swansea, Singleton Park, Swansea, SA2 8PP. (Magazine of criticism which now uses increasing amount of poetry in all styles. Contributions from outside Wales welcome.)

Valleys Poet, Eugene Nowakowski, 123 Coedpenmaen Road, Pontypridd, Mid-Glamorgan, CF37 4LH. (Classic little mag of mainly valleys poetry but open to all. *Cardiff Poet* magazine published by the same editor.)

The Works, 11 Wingate Drive, Llanishen, Cardiff, CF4 5LR. (The Welsh Union of Writers' occasional journal of poetry, prose and criticism from Wales.)

Chapter Two

Competitions

The late Howard Sergeant, editor of one of Britain's longest running small magazines, *Outposts*, had a theory that poetry in the UK was controlled by the equivalent of a literary mafia. This cartel, he claimed, originated in the big universities, all members knew each other personally, reviewed each others' books, and all were editors of something — a magazine, a publishing house, a radio show, or even a literary events programme. Their names revolved on an inner wheel of success, turning up in most of poetry's outlets again and again. This clique, he said, consisted of only a few dozen individuals and although membership had been known to change it did so rarely. You had to be the poetical equivalent of a mason to get in. This may be exaggerating the position somewhat but a lot of poets in this country share Howard Sergeant's views. How on earth do you break in? Craig Raine, Andrew Motion, Wendy Cope, John Fuller, Ted Hughes, Tony Curtis, Gillian Clarke — the names of those who have succeeded spin around us. The fact that they may actually be talented rarely occurs to those complaining. It is plot and intrigue that got them where they are. We are not published by *The Independent* and the *TLS* because we are outsiders. Our poems don't make it onto Radio 3 because our names are wrong.

Poetry competitions appear to offer a way out of this impasse. They are the universal literary panacea of the 90s. Look at the winners of some of the bigger contests: Asher F. Mendelssohn, Monica Ditmas, Fergus Chadwick, Christopher J. Gleed, Roland Porchmouth — who are these people? Have you heard of them? The system obviously works. Competitions are entered anonymously — your poems go into the same heap as those by Peter Redgrove, Tom Paulin, Carol Rumens and for all you know Allen Ginsberg, R.S. Thomas and Helen Steiner Rice. The judges — usually a panel of writers like Wendy Cope, Anthony Thwaite and Fleur Adcock — are required to decide which poems succeed on merit alone. The editorial forces which grant publication according to who you are and where you live don't come into it. The winning verses go forward as a result of what they say and how they are constructed alone.

The Bardic Contest — How Does It Work?

We should be used to this idea of bardic competition in Wales with our tradition of eisteddfod combat, but most still find the concept of metrical contests a little odd. Not that there is much to be won either. One recent local eisteddfod was seen to be offering prizes in the range of 80p, 60p and 40p — admittedly for recitation rather than writing. If you composed your own then you were in for a little more — a book-token for five pounds. Most English language competitions offer if not the kudos, then at least a financial reward worth having — usually hundreds of pounds.

The whole thing works like a vanity version of the football pools. The poet, self-assured enough with his or her own creation, pays the few pounds entry fee and the poems all go into a pot. The best rise to the surface to claim the prizes. The organisers pay the judges their slab and then keep what remains as profit. In a survey I carried out recently almost all organizers admitted that their prime motivation was making money. A few, like the Welsh Academy, saw competitions as part of their brief to promote literature but even they are making small sums from their first rate City of Cardiff International Competition.

It's a gamble. You bet money on yourself and if the odds are with you then you win. How can it be any more than this? Can different poems really compete against each other? Even the judges sometimes have their doubts.

> They stretched a never-ending line ... haikus, ballads, sonnets, epics, allegories, elegies, epistles, prophecies, fantasies, litanies, formal, experimental, propagandist, confessional, surreal, satirical, narrative, encyclopaedic, obscene, primitive, artful, anguished... how to balance long poems — some of them running to 90 pages — against short lyrics, how to decide between technical sophistication and authentic feeling, between the exquisite and the ambitious? It was a long haul. — Seamus Heaney and Ted Hughes from their introduction to the *Arvon 1980* anthology.

THE POETRY BUSINESS

When did it all start?

Local societies have run competitions for decades — 25p a go, total of 30 entries, first prize a rosette. *The Felicia Hemans Prize for Lyrical Poetry* for example — offers winners no more than a bronze medal. The Poetry Society's *Greenwood Prize* is slightly more adventurous — here the prize is £20. The really big competitons offering large rewards however — specifically those run by the Arvon Foundation and the *National Poetry Competition* run by the Poetry Society — didn't start until the end of the 70s. The response to them was enormous. From out of the woodwork came thousands and thousands of new poets, far more than anyone had imagined existed. The 1980 Arvon attracted 35,000 poems and 33,000 in 1982. The National drew 16,000. If only all these people bought books then poetry could become truly commercial overnight. The prizes were on a similar grand scale: £1000, £2000, £5000. Enough money to feed half of Africa for one poem.

Competitions began to spring up all over the place. Existing contests upped their rewards. The *Arvon Foundation National Poetry Competition*, run in cahoots with *The Observer*, and the *Poetry Society's National* run with the help of Radio 3 were joined by the *Peterloo Poets Open* sponsored by Marks and Spencer (£2000 first prize), *The Poetry Digest Bard of the Year* (one thousand guineas plus a crown), *Bridport Arts Centre* (£1000), *The Cardiff Literature Festival Competition* — sponsor Cardiff City Council (£1000), *Orbis Competition For Rhyming Poetry* (£1000), *The X.E. Nathan Open Poetry Award* (£1500) and many others. Local contests spread like an epidemic of flu. Magazines, writers clubs, charities and specialist bookshops all seemed to be in on the game of offering prizes to bards — £30 and a selection of books from *Tabla Poetry Magazine*, £100 and life subscription to the magazine from *The Frogmore Papers*, £50 from West Sussex Writer's Club.

The poets responded with streams of bland, immediate-impact versifying — a kind of unobjectionable, middle-ground poetry seemed to be just what most judges wanted. Comments Sheenagh Pugh, both a winner and a judge, "I have come to the conclusion that there is a type of competition poem — fairly short and with some quality of instant 'memorability' about it". Stark individuality is not what works here. For all competitions other than the Arvon, which seems to thrive on peculiarity, it pays to be as conventional as hell.

Competitions Now

Today the peak has passed. All the big competitions report a drop in overall entry since the mid-80s. Gillian Clarke, a judge of long standing, is certain that the market is now saturated. Has this stopped anyone? Not a bit of it. The other day I spoke to a scout group leader who was thinking of initiating a limerick contest, the week before it was a brewery considering how best to get poets to write about beer. Lancaster Literature Festival announce their latest — the top thirty winners all get an equal prize of £20 plus publication in the festival anthology. Variations are endless, the list goes on and on. Where is the best place to spend two pounds? Not on a competition, I'd say, but on a poetry magazine — but then I'm biased.

A lot of writers actually consider competitions to be wrong in principle. "They are sheer, naked, money-making ventures. It is no coincidence that they have grown to prominence during Thatcherism. They encourage new writing, most of which is bad," says Robert Minhinnick. Others don't like them for more personal reasons. Fleur Adcock won't enter them because she doesn't "want to be placed 57th", Dannie Abse is no fan either mainly because he feels he also may not win. Robert Minhinnick admits he tried once and wasn't placed. I always maintain that I never bother although the truth is that I once did, a long time ago and, full of expectation, found myself not even mentioned among the also rans.

But this fear of unexplained failure doesn't stop some writers of reputation trying their hand — Peter Redgrove, Tony Curtis, Oliver Reynolds, Philip Gross, Tony Harrison, Hugo Williams, Andrew Motion, U.A. Fanthorpe, Pete Morgan, Andrew Waterman and Anne Stevenson are among those who have entered and come out on top.

Which comps do you try? The big ones offer the glittering prizes but the odds are long. A number of prominent poets are reputed not to enter when the prize dips to less than £500 for fear of demeaning themselves. This would leave the field clear for the rest of us quite content with a detrimental £350 or even a degrading £50 if it comes to that. Smaller shows, like smaller magazines, offer a better bet for the beginner.

Do you want to do do this? How to make up your mind.

What you have to decide is:

1) What good will winning do you? Will being able to say you were a runner up in the *Aberdulais and District Writers Circle Anniversary Contest* do you any good? How will that embellish your life or your cv?

2) How much does it cost to enter and how much are you likely to win?

3) Is publication of any sort involved? Many contests have anthologies of prize winners. Others ensure publication in reputable literary magazines. For some poets this itself will justify entering.

4) Is criticism offered? Some of the smaller competitions get their judges to offer remarks on every entry. Do you want this?

5) Do you want to tie up your long slaved-over work for anything up to 18 months in order that it remain unpublished, a precondition of entry for most competitions?

6) What other advantages could writing offer you? Sheenagh Pugh again: "If you win you can get a lot of publicity, though whether that is reflected in book sales depends entirely on whether your publisher makes any use of it — the day I came to collect the prize for the *Poem for Today* competition, I checked the Cardiff bookshops and only one had my collection, then not long published". On the other hand your photo in the local paper may be reward enough. You decide.

7) Can you really be bothered? Isn't subscribing to *Poetry Wales* and then sending your work in (£20 or so paid on publication) much the same kind of thing?

COMPETITIONS

What Kind of Poems Win?

What will the judges like? Vernon Scannell, a judge in the 1983 National, offers this advice on what not to send: "Far too much greeting-card doggerel was submitted by writers who clearly had never looked at a real poem. The other easily rejected category presented the kind of poem — written either in a traditional but entirely mechanical metric or in flaccid 'free verse' — that was packed with abstractions such as *Time, Life, Soul, Beauty* and so on which were named but never embodied". Tony Curtis, Wales' greatest success in the field, keeps his formula for winning close to his chest although he did let slip once while prowling the bookshop shelves that he always reads the judges' own work before entering. Enough said.

Where To Find Out More:

Appendix III lists UK competitions known to have been running during the past two years or so.

The Poetry Library publish a free 'Selective List of Poetry Competitions' which is updated monthly. Send SAE to the library at Royal Festival Hall, South Bank Centre, London, SE1 8XX.

Guide to Literary Prizes, Grants and Awards in Britain and Ireland contains information for those who really want to get to the top. Published by *Book Trust* (45 East Hill, London, SW18 2QZ).

The following magazines all have good coverage of current competitions:

Freelance Writing & Photography, John T. Wilson, Weavers Press Publishing, Tregeraint House, Zennor, St Ives, Cornwall, TR26 3DB.
Orbis, Mike Shields, 199 The Long Shoot, Nuneaton, Warwickshire, CV11 6JA.
Quartos, BCM Writer, London, WC1N 3XX.
Writers' Monthly, 29 Turnpike Lane, London, N8 OEP.
Writers News, PO Box 4, Nairn, IV12 4HU.

THE POETRY BUSINESS

In Wales the newsletters of both the Welsh Academy, *BWA*, (Third Floor, Mount Stuart House, Mount Stuart Square, Docks, Cardiff CF1 6DQ) and the Welsh Union of Writers, *WUW News*, (11 Wingate Drive, Cardiff, CF4 5LR) list current competitions. Further afield information can also be obtained from your library (check out the noticeboard and the leaflet racks) as well as from your local arts board.

Chapter Three

The Reading

The platform, the lectern, the jug of water, the small expectant audience. At some point in your writing career you are going to come up against this — the poetry reading. For a few it will be a moment to savour, a chance to get up there in the spotlight and show what you're made of. This is the one occasion in the poetry business where instant reactions are possible — applause, laughter, murmurs of acknowledgement. You stand there recollecting your emotions in tranquillity and if it works you find out straight away. Readings provide immediate feedback.

But for most of us it will be an ordeal. Speaking before a group rates high in the survey of human fears — well above sickness, death and flying, even above money trouble, spiders and bugs. Being a poet does not automatically make you an actor but here you are called upon to give public performances. What is it all about?

Vernon Scannell has it in his book *How To Enjoy Poetry* (Piatkus): "To hear a good poet read his work aloud, even if he is not an accomplished public speaker, is a valuable guide to where precise emphases are to be placed...The principal justification for popular recitals of poetry...is that audiences will come to associate poetry with pleasure and not feel that it is an act available only to an initiate minority". Readings extend both the range of the poem, the presence of the poet and can help demystify the art. Of course, poetry was originally a spoken activity. In the days before printed books, verse was used as a mnemonic — heroic tales were chanted, the fall of kings recounted; poetry was much closer to song. Nonetheless readings as we now think of them can hardly be said to have existed before the twentieth century and there is some evidence that they predominate only in the latter half. Both Glyn Jones and Raymond Garlick, beginning to write in the 30s and 40s respectively, report that poetry readings were non-existent when they started out.

THE POETRY BUSINESS

Are They Worth Doing?

You are not going to go far in the poetry world today without encountering readings, yet not everyone is convinced of their usefulness. The late John Ormond was suspicious of what could happen if the poet made too much of a play for the audience. "To write for public reading is to move the making towards writing for theatre; and it *can* lead to empty rhetoric, worse still".

Raymond Garlick expresses his misgivings in verse:

> Poetry is the written word,
> Black upon white, read before heard;
> Precise inscription of the heart,
> Not a brash performing art.
> Poems stir the page's breast —
> Hearing them is second best.
> (From *Notes for an Autobiography*)

Not everyone agrees. The 1980s saw a massive upsurge in the interest in performed poetry in all its variants — dub, rant, rap, — as opposed to straight recitations — and a number of writers have emerged whose whole raison d'être is the live poem. Ifor Thomas, Ivor Cutler, Adrian Mitchell, Joolz, Benjamin Zephaniah, Henry Normal, Attila The Stockbroker, Linton Kwesi Johnson, Bridgit Bard, Brother Resistance, Bob Cobbing and others all work best when you hear them; they write with that in mind. Pitch yourself where you like between the two extremes. Dannie Abse, Wales' live reader par excellence, reckons that, anyway, half the enjoyment of a poetry reading is the social event and the poet's comments between poems. It's a literary night out, a chance to meet others of a like mind.

Cash

Poetry readings are undoubtedly the poet's best way of making money. Poetry itself actually pays very little. The odd pound for a poem included in one of the better magazines, a miserly royalty if you get a collection published and maybe £10 here and £20 there for an anthology appearance. Readings offer better rewards. The standard minimum fee at present is around £40 per appearance which many poets still do not regard as anything like enough. Beginners should expect to offer their services for much less until they are practised in the art.

Audiences

The business runs in cycles. There are surges of interest, and at present we would seem to be at the tail end of a big one. The last time poetry was as popular as this was in the 60s with the great Albert Hall Poetry Show starring Allen Ginsberg, and the Cardiff Commonwealth Poetry Conference with poets shooting arrows at breakfast in the Park Hotel, multinational bards drunk in the lifts and live pigs performing at the Reardon Smith. Recent events have pulled huge audiences too — Linton Kwesi Johnson at the Sherman Theatre, Poetry for May Day in the 70s, Ted Hughes and Thom Gunn in Cardiff, R.S. Thomas at the Oriel Bookshop. But there have been disasters as well. James Simmons, a first class Irish writer and an excellent performer, attracted two people to his reading in the Vale of Glamorgan. Paula Claire and her leek chants managed a similar number in Cardiff. Organizers seem never to be sure quite what will work.

I've no way of proving this but I suspect that audiences at readings are of pretty much the same composition as those for the books themselves — friends of the poet reading, other poets, the companions of the other poets plus the odd teacher, arts administrator and academic. Get the event on the wrong night or mishandle the publicity and you are lost. Interests are so specific that if there is a conflicting programme on television the poetry reading audience can turn out to be nil.

Style

These things have a style of their own. They are not lectures or piano recitals. Formality is hardly ever a reading's strong point. This is often mistaken for amateurishness but by now it is so common that it is part of the tradition. There are a thousand difficulties to contend with. Chairpeople who don't know the names of the poets, noises off, dogs, people arriving late, not enough seats, drunken poets who fall asleep, or off the platform, or once at a famous event I attended in the Guildhall or some such in Leicester actually into a blazing iron-basketed fire; poets who are not satisfied with the size of their audiences — Alan Bold in Cardiff in the 60s decided that the dedicated assembled in the lounge were not enough and so moved en masse into the public bar where the dart throwers and cribbage players had to put up with him whether they liked it or not. Some poets are bad value for money — ask them for half an hour and they do twenty minutes and then rush off for the train. Others are worse — they go on for hours taking up at first all the space allocated for co-readers and then that set aside at the end for drinking or for selling books. Sometimes the organizers have competely fouled it up — put on the event in direct competition with another, not done adequate or any promotion, failed to book a room of decent size or neglected to even provide an mc.

> 'Where do you want me to read?'
> 'Oh, anywhere. Just stand up.'
> 'And will you be introducing me?'
> 'I hadn't thought to. Can't you say something yourself?'

The reading on a wrong night excuse for poor turnout is now classic:

> If you had come on a Monday,
> or a Tuesday, or a Thursday
> If you had come on a Wednesday,
> or any day but this,
> You would have had an audience.
> (Louis Simpson — 'Before The Poetry Reading')

Yet despite these hazards many readings can be memorable: John Ashbery's cool wit at Cardiff Art College, Al Purdy and Alan Perry's poem balancing tour de force at St Donat's, John Agard's dynamic performance at Oriel.

Wales has produced its fair share of excellent readers — Dylan Thomas, whose voice and whole approach to reading is claimed by some to have started the thing off, and John Tripp, a writer who knew exactly what his audience wanted and gave it to them. Current professionals of the first order include Leslie Norris, Dannie Abse, Tony Curtis and Gillian Clarke — all good value for money when it comes to the traditional reading. For the cutting edge of performance you'll need to listen to groups like Undercover, Horse's Mouth, Chris Torrance's Poet Heat, and Deadlier Than The Male.

How Do You Start?

From the new writer's standpoint how do you break in? Who invites you? How do you get up there and start wowing your neighbours? Vernon Scannell has one answer: You don't. "The poet who is dedicated to his craft...which involves compressing the maximum amount of passion, thought, wit and vision into the smallest possible space and achieving rhythmic effects of great variety and subtlety, is unlikely to be appreciated by an audience which is probably encountering his work for the first time". Yet some writers whose writing methods roughly follow this description regard the reading as part of their stock in trade: Roger McGough, Jeremy Reed, Robert Minhinnick. Even R.S. Thomas, once a rare public performer, has been on the road a fair bit recently. If you enjoy direct communication then the reading is for you.

How Do You Do It?

You should practise. Try into the cassette recorder, in front of the bathroom mirror, in the kitchen. Whatever you do make sure you've tried the thing out loud before you appear in public. Glyn Jones thinks "poets reading ought to be as professional as performing musicians". Try for this. Watch out for stumbles, make sure the copy you're to read from is clear. Stage performers will tell you that the links between items are often as important as the items themselves. Prepare the odd anecdote, work up a programme, time it so you don't over-run. Use the advice from the Music Hall — the poetry reading is often very similar — don't wave your arms around, keep to one spot, keep your face straight, don't drink on stage, don't drop your papers, know what you are going to do next, and look the audience in the eye — this is vital and politicians know it — eye to eye contact adds sincerity, cements communication. Don't read to that spot at the back of the room. Talk to the people who have come to hear you. Take time and trouble. You are there because you have something to give. This is the way.

THE POETRY BUSINESS

It is best to forget initially all that you've heard about learning by rote and reciting your work from memory — although some performance poets use this to advantage. Speak plainly in your natural voice. Histrionics can come later. If you are really worried listen to Dylan Thomas' recordings, go to poetry readings — especially any put on in London by Apples & Snakes whose anthology, *The Popular Front Of Contemporary Poetry*, sums the whole scene up (Unit A11, Hatcham Mews Centre, Hatcham Park Mews, London, SE14 5QA. Tel: 071 639 9656). You might also care to listen out for anything organised under the Poetry Olympics banner by master of the anglo-saxophone Mike Horovitz (Piedmont, Bisley, Stroud, Gloucestershire, GL6 7BU). For information on classical presentation read Betty Mulcahy's *How To Speak a Poem* (Autolycus Press £6.95).

"Make sure you are writing good work first; not easy, and not a quick task." — John Ormond. Ultimately Glyn Jones advises: "Be ready to recognise that poetry readings may not be for you. Reading poetry successfully presupposes, ideally, a good voice, a presence, an actor's out-going personality that can dominate or intrigue an audience — and how many poets are like that?" Nonetheless if you write well you should try. Best get your practice in now.

Getting invited to read somewhere is really a bit like getting your first collection accepted. It is a matter of reputation, who you know, and how far you are willing to push yourself. Start with the open readings put on by local writing groups; contact your Regional Arts Board and make sure they know that you are looking for work; attend mainstream readings and make certain the organizers get to know who you are; contact the Welsh Union of Writers and the Welsh Academy to see if they can help you. Write to the organizers of the Hay, Clwyd Libraries and Cardiff Literature festivals. Make sure artistic boss of Swansea City of Literature, Sean Doran, knows who you are. Prepare a cv on yourself and send it round. Tape yourself performing and send a cassette to the BBC, to festival organizers, to the local library. The certain will enter the *John Tripp Award For Spoken Poetry* organized by the Welsh Academy with sponsorship from Glengettie Tea. Heats are held throughout Wales — a £5 entry fee gets you ten minutes in front the judges. The best at the finals wins £1000 plus an antique tea pot. BP a few years back ran a similar contest at the South Bank, London. If all else fails then promote yourself. Be bold. Book the church hall and invite yourself to read. Such approaches work. The late John Ormond, however, always distrusted the self-promoters: "most of those whose names are always on the top of the heap in every event they run themselves, are the egoists and the self-seekers", and he was right for much of the time. Yet not all poets do it just for the ego — for many it is part of the art. It generates interest, it sells books, it keeps you working. You might even enjoy the experience.

Contact Addresses:

Welsh Academy and the *Cardiff Literature Festival*, Third Floor, Mount Stuart House, Mount Stuart Square, Cardiff, CF1 6DQ. Tel: 0222 492025.

Swansea City Of Literature 1995, Somerset Place, Swansea, SA1 1SE. Tel: 0792 480211.

Hay-on-Wye Festival of Literature, Peter Florence, Festival Box Office, Hay-on-Wye, HR3 5BX. Tel: 0497 821299.

Arts Council of Wales Regional Offices:

North Wales office, 10 Wellfield House, Bangor, Gwynedd, LL57 1ER. Tel: 0248 353248.
West Wales office, 3 Heol Goch, Carmarthen, Dyfed, SA31 1QL. Tel: 0267 234248.
South East Wales office, Victoria Street, Cwmbran, Gwent, NP44 3YT. Tel: 0633 875075.
North East Wales office, Daniel Owen Centre, Earl Road, Mold, Clwyd, CH7 1AP. Tel: 0352 758403.

Arts Council of Wales main office:

Arts Council of Wales, Museum Place, Cardiff, CF1 3NX. Tel: 0222 394711.

Chapter Four

Groups of Poets
Circles, Classes, Courses And
Societies For The Writer

I was surprised to discover recently while researching for something else that a fair number of the general public regard writers as peculiar. Now let's qualify this: I don't mean the *general* general public, I mean the book-reading, potentially creative general public. This broadly middle-class section of society, it seems, have their suspicions not so much about writers as a whole but more about *poets*. Novelists and suchlike they can handle, they are in all the shops and appear on tv, but poets — these people are infinitely strange.

I come into contact with a lot of writers on a daily basis and I agree that as a breed they are not significantly peculiar. The professionals for the most part are professional — and the gifted amateurs, particularly here in Wales, are generally straight up and down. But the poets are something else. Out here on the fringes non-conformity abounds. For many embarking on a career in verse unconventionality becomes a prerequisite. To get ahead one must be odd. Great poets are all seen as mad people leading magnificent, drunken, bohemian lives. These traits are so obviously the route to visionary creation that they must be imitated. People forget that T.S. Eliot was a quiet businessman and that Vernon Watkins, direct from the first age of Anglo-Welsh debauchery, worked in a bank.

Contemporary poets seem to apply themselves with gusto to their lifestyles. For at least forty years, and especially after Dylan Thomas went to America, we have had to suffer oddly dressed literary philanderers falling off stages, hailing taxis with wine carafes, being unable to speak, standing on mantelpieces, burning the books of their rivals, riding around bookshops on bicycles, being drunk, being incomprehensibly drunk, being so drunk that they had to be moved by railway trolleys, dressing as gorillas, crossing cities on roof-racks, giving impromptu readings on aeroplanes, being sick on television, eating money, appearing nude in public, graffitoing, masquerading as politicians, urinating on street fires, not paying their fines and spending time in prison.

The advent of the performance poem has not helped things. Professional poets are now required to wrap themselves in cling-film, flail at furniture with chainsaws, yell through loudhailers, swing across auditoria on ropes and appear at venues dressed as anything from a camel to a cardboard box.

It's great fun, of course, but it can turn into a bit of a circus and not all practitioners enjoy being in the ring. Many actually abhor stage performance altogether and won't go much further than reading to a quiet group in a local hall. Most poets are underneath pretty conventional — they watch *Neighbours*, they drink beer, they go for family holidays in the sun.

What does have to be remembered is that once the surface distraction has been removed and the surging ego channelled into actual creation then what remains is hard work. Poetry does not come easy. Despite what you might read in the books of some poets, mine included, poetry is rarely found lying around.

Almost certainly the single most effective way of improving how you write is to read the work of others. Another is to somehow get others to read yours. The place where this can best be achieved is the writers' group, the poets' club or the creative writing evening class. Such exercises are no substitute for familiarity with the work of acknowledged masters but attending the odd meeting is bound to help.

Societies For Writers

Writers' societies come in all shapes, styles and sizes. They range from the august *Dylan Thomas Society* which concentrates on the work of the great bard, the biannual *SAMWAW* (South and Mid Wales Association of Writers) conventions held over long weekends at Duffryn House, Cardiff, and Anne Hobbs' *Writers Holidays* which keep 200 scribes fully occupied for a week each year at Harlech, to local associations of a dozen or so who meet monthly at the local pub. Poetry is not always that high on the agenda. One of *SAMWAW*'s recent conferences offered delegates a choice between verse with Guyanian poet Fred d'Aguiar and format romance writing with a team of editors from Mills & Boon. The mass market won hands down with over eighty per cent deciding that their pulp writing abilities were more in need of help than their verse. The same sort of thing is often true of the many writers' circles across Wales which, by their choice of the now old fashioned appellation 'circle', reveal their longevity. These societies tend to service the middle-aged writer keen on placing articles in journals, selling stories to radio and writing genre novels. Poets do fit in here but their activities play a minor part.

The more recently formed societies sometimes call themselves things like *Noumena*, or *Undercover*, but more often plump for the generic term 'writers', as in *Upper Colwyn Bay Writers* or *Tondu Writers' Workshop*. Here will be found a more enthusiastic attitude towards poetry with a few such as *The Gwent Poetry Society* and *The Stow Hill Poets* devoting themselves exclusively to verse.

The only real way to discover a group's bias is to attend. Writers' societies are very much flavoured by their principal members — some are open, welcoming, easy to get heard at while others seem to require a kind of masonic initiation by the casual visitor before they are allowed to take part.

The broad system of operation is generally the same. The group meets on a regular basis. There is a chairperson to control the meeting, and local practice decides whether this should be rigid and formal or if anything will go. During meetings members are given a chance to read out their work and others to criticize. With the addition of occasional talks by specialists, guest readings by poets and the passing on of information concerning the literary world this seems to be why most people come. Rarely are participants academically qualified for the process but this matters little. Criticism is intended to be constructive. Those receiving it go home full of new ideas about how the poem should be re-written or indeed how a fresh one could be formed.

Groups are not all ice cream however. Author Michael Baldwin offers this warning:

> Writers' circles attract the smug and the self-protective. They also encourage the dozy dogmatist; but it should only take one person of genuine will to bring the warring egos into a focus. All that is required ultimately is that people should listen to each other, grant a platform in return for a platform. It is good to temper our poetry in fierce, even wild or ribald criticism. To be read to a circle is often

our poem's first publication. To hear it criticised will be depressing, stimulating, exasperating in turns — but at least we will see our work through others' eyes, and pick our way through valid and invalid comment.

The Way To Write Poetry — Elm Tree Books.

The Creative Writing Class

A variant on the standard writers group is the tutor-led writing class. The American idea that creative writing should be taught to adults took Wales by storm in 1981, when the Welsh Academy set up a number of creative writing workshops for the unemployed. It soon became apparent that the need for guidance in the arts of writing was not limited to those out of work and demand began to outstrip supply. Requests from across the social spectrum led to the establishment of workshops, local authority evening classes, extra mural and tutorial groups throughout Wales. Some specialized in specific genres such as theatre writing or novels, while others were directed at groups specified by race, gender, disability, language or sexual preference. The boom in writers' workshops for women has been considerable. Most new ventures, including the many now being established by the public library system, show a healthy concern for poetry.

Tutor-run classes differ from standard writers' groups mainly in the matter of leadership. The elements described earlier are all present but guided by a tutor, usually a writer of some experience, who supplements the expected exchange of new work with a number of more formal sessions where new concepts are introduced and techniques actually taught.

From an array of successful creative writing teachers for this kind of adult class which has included at various times poets as diverse as Nigel Jenkins, Sally Roberts Jones, Duncan Bush, Graham Hartill, Phil Maillard, Gillian Clarke, Gill Brightmore, Menna Elfyn and Tony Curtis, one figure emerges as outstanding: Chris Torrance, a sort of backwoods preacher of poetry, has run the almost legendary *Adventures in Creative Writing* for the extra-mural department in Cardiff since the 70s. His approach to tutoring is extremely open with plenty of opportunity for poets of all kinds. Styles are unlimited. Censorship of form is not practised and literary foreknowledge is not required. The class has earned a reputation for being the friendliest in Wales.

Torrance, replete with knitted hat and flask of hot tea like a man out to feed the ducks on Roath Park Lake, concentrates on getting things going. "My first step is to get them writing and keep them writing. I believe that exercising the machinery of writing is much more important than intensive literary analysis and 'lit-crit', which tends to frighten away people unfamliar with this mode...This is not to say that critical discussion doesn't go on in the class; it goes on all the time, although a better word for it is discourse". Chris Torrance has also identified perhaps the most significant benefit of all this literary fraternization: that "*Writers need to get together*. To profess interest in writing especially poetry is to often draw down scorn from one's immediate social and familial circle: to go from that situation into one where writing is *the* topic and where all present are trying to write should and usually does prove stimulating."

Some tutors take the view, however, that not all of this is really worthwhile. What figures of significance have emerged from the classes during this past decade who, had there not been a class to attend, would not have succeeded anyway? Duncan Bush suspects that "in the so called civilized world writing groups have a more social or therapeutic than literary value for most of the members and are of more financial than literary value to the tutors". His suspicions are not unfamiliar and it may well be that creative writing is no more than a kind of 90s basket weaving — keeping us all occupied while the Japanese-inspired industrial machine earns our bread. He continues: "Education to trash is so much a part of our culture now that it's a nonsense to expect people to know good from bad in such superannuated areas of skill or pleasure as reading and writing. Until this problem is addressed, you can have a writing group on every corner and it still won't throw up writing that's really fit to print". Yet much of this depends where you stand. Is there really a need for more writers? Don't we have enough anyway? Or could it be that the teaching of the skills to write poetry will actually increase the demand for the stuff itself? Since most poetry is at present consumed by its practitioners I suspect this latter point to be so. In any event, if you have decided you want to write poetry then tuition is more likely to be of help to you than sky sent bolts of inspiration. Your group will provide you with an audience at very least.

Many successful workshops go on to publish magazines of their work and to put on public readings. *Gob-Stoppers, Cabaret 246, Madoc, Green Pens, Writing On Air, Deadlier Than The Male* are all either the direct products of writing classes or were begun that way. Poetry workshops are an all round route to improvement. As Torrance says "writers' groups produce...a general grassroots togetherness that gives the individual writer his or her chance to come out of isolation". Playing games like how many words can you think of to describe winter, or completing poems begun by others and finding subjects, key words or part sequences by pulling them out of a hat does lead somewhere. Writers' groups in themselves do not necessarily produce world-class writers but belonging to one will certainly improve both your poetry composition and perhaps more importantly your attitude to poetry. It will show you that you are not unique, for a start.

How do you find out about local groups? Check Appendix IV which lists groups in Wales, send for one of the three regional newsletters listed below or ring your local arts office. Check the noticeboards in the library for new initiatives. Jill Dick's *Writers' Circles* published by Laurence Pollinger Ltd, 18 Maddox Street, Mayfair, London, W1R 0EU lists hundreds of groups throughout the UK. If there is no local group then why not start one? It takes only a small amount of organizational ability and you're away. Certainly you should join one of the two big Welsh organizations for writers — the Welsh Academy and the Welsh Union of Writers. Both are able to provide you with help, advice and information as well as to put you in touch with fellow members of a similar mind. Don't hesitate. Join Now.

Should you have the time (and possibly the money) you might also consider trying a residential week under the tuition of first rate professional poets. In Wales the Taliesin Trust at Tŷ Newydd, and in England the Arvon Foundation at Lumb Bank and Totleigh Barton, and in Scotland at Moniack Mhor, run courses on a regular basis. The system is more or less the same in all four centres — a dozen or so students gather in a country house for an intense period of writing, instruction, discussion and retreat. It is an experience not to be missed. All centres produce their own brochures; send a sae for more information. Those who are interested in making writing their career might look at the two new MAs in Creative Writing offered by the University of Glamorgan and by the University of Wales, College of Cardiff. Glamorgan's course offers a two-year part-time Master of Arts degree for writers of fiction and poetry. It is based on the distance learning principle. Payment of fees, currently £1000 per annum, is by direct debit, as you learn, and attendance at the campus is only necessary for certain key workshops. Tuition is by post. Tutors include poets Tony Curtis, Christopher Meredith, Gillian Clarke, Helen Dunmore and Sheenagh Pugh. The MA at Cardiff is slightly different. This offers a Master's degree in the Teaching and Practice of Creative Writing and is taught on a weekly basis for a year. Students will be assessed on their portfolios of writing which will include four special projects. Tutors include the poets Norman Schwenk, John Freeman and Anne Cluysenaar. For more information write to the addresses below.

Contact addresses:

The Taliesin Trust at Tŷ Newydd, Llanystumdwy, Cricieth, Gwynedd, LL52 0LW. Tel: 0766 522811.

The Arvon Foundation at Totleigh Barton, Sheepwash, Devon, EX21 5NS; at Lumb Bank, Heptonstall, Hebden Bridge, West Yorkshire, HX7 6DF; and at Moniack Mhor, Moniack, Inverness, IV5 7PQ.

University of Glamorgan, School of Humanities and Social Sciences, Treforest, Pontypridd, Mid Glamorgan, CF37 1DL. Tel: 0443 482551.

University of Wales, College of Cardiff, School of English Studies, PO Box 94, Cardiff, CF1 3XB. Tel: 0222 874241.

Welsh Academy, Third Floor, Mount Stuart House, Mount Stuart Square, Docks, Cardiff, CF1 6DQ.

Welsh Union of Writers, 11 Wingate Drive, Llanishen, Cardiff, CF4 5LR.

News of Welsh Writers' Groups Can be Found in the Following:

New Lines (North Wales), Joe Kelly, PO Box 658, Mold, Clwyd, CH7 1FB.

West Wales Writers' Umbrella Literature Newsletter, Y Garn, Swansea Road, Llewitha, Fforestfach, Swansea, West Glamorgan, SA5 4NR.

South East Literature Events, Bob Mole, South East Wales Arts Office, Victoria Street, Cwmbran, Gwent, NP44 3YT.

GROUPS OF POETS

The British Council also publish two annual directories useful to poets:

Literature and Creative Writing: Short Courses and Summer Schools In Britain.
Postgraduate Study in British Literature.

Both are available from 10 Spring Gardens, London, SW1A 2BN.

Chapter Five

Bringing Out Your First Book

A re you sure you want to do this? Just because you write does not mean that you have to publish the stuff. Certainly you may have dabbled at readings and made the odd magazine appearance but a collection of poems, a whole book devoted just to you — this is a major undertaking. Sir Thomas More, as long ago as 1515, was unsure if the effort was really worth it. "Tastes differ so widely, and some people are so humourless, so uncharitable, and so absurdly wrong-headed, that one would probably do far better to relax and enjoy life than worry oneself to death trying to instruct or entertain a public which will only despise one's efforts, or at least feel no gratitude for them."

Anyway, there are so many new books finding there way onto the market — more than 60,000 in the UK alone last year — that it seems nothing short of foolhardy to try to add to them. Why increase the agony? Even in Wales there are more new poetry books around than I've seen in years. There is a boom on. But a boom in publishing, it seems, not reading. Most new poetry titles still sell less than 400 copies. A school magazine will do better. Considered against potential circulation, 400 is a miserable achievement. Publishers of blockbuster biography send out that many copies as complimentaries.

Ezra Pound, one of the founders of literary modernism, wanted to "make the Italian Renaissance look like a tempest in a teapot". His poetry was to be a vehicle of revolutionary change. "If one is going to print opinions the public already agrees with," he wrote, "what is the use of printing them at all? Good art cannot be palatable all at once". Unfortunately most writers do not like disagreement. The contemporary cabal seem bent on keeping things as palatable as possible. They fear for their readership, I suppose, yet their actions have had a minimal effect on sales, if at all.

It is the excesses of Pound's followers, of course, which have made the buying public suspicious. There is a long history of readers being confused and outraged by what has been served up to them as poetry. Poetry has been, as Sally Dennison puts it, "freed of end rhymes and strict rhythms. Ambiguity and uncertainty made virtues and form turned fluid to support a fluid content...prudery has been banished in favour of honesty...conventions have been trampled down". To some it has appeared as if anything is acceptable. Poetry is easy, you just do it, but the true situation is a bit more complex than that.

Personally I would like to see a public educated into putting more effort into their reading. Not all good things are as obvious as a chocolate box lid; not everything worth hearing will shout in your ear. However, I have come to terms with the fact that this is not to be. The largest group of readers of contemporary poetry, anyway, turn out to be the poets themselves, late twentieth century traditionalists looking for acceptability, fame and sales. The business windmills in the mist. In the real world people sit at home watching tv.

Despite all of this, experience shows that trying to dissuade poets from attempting to publish their first collections is about as successful as keeping Nigel Jenkins out of the bar. There is something about a first book with your name on the cover which is irresistible. First books are unbelievable. Writers hold them for hours at a stretch, study them, feel their covers, put them in their pockets and then pull them out again just to be sure that the print is still there. I kept a copy of *Wanted For Writing Poetry*, my first pamphlet, in every room of my flat. Visitors would be hard put not to notice it. When the Jehovahs called pushing the *Watchtower* I responded by fighting back with my verse. We ended by swopping. Doggerel for dogma as it turned out, but I thought it was wonderful at the time. First books have a quality which cannot be repeated. They show that at last you've made it, put yourself in company with all the other real writers of the world. You are complete with ISBN and barcode, listed on Bookbank's CD-ROM, available in the British Library, purchasable, orderable, readable. The facts that you are also remainderable, pulpable, forgetable and possibly even incomprehensible don't cross your mind at all.

To become published, the simple desire to communicate, the need to entertain or even the compulsion to commit art with your verse need to be strengthened by the push of the ego. Succeed or bust. Get the book out. Your first book will give you confidence as a writer. Lots of exciting things will suddenly start to happen. Robert Morgan found that following the appearance of his *The Night's Prison*, he had "poems broadcast, readings everywhere, many poems in all kinds of magazines and even a short film shown on Southern tv". Penny Windsor, who reckons she held herself back for 32 years before bringing out *Heroines*, says that its appearance "in terms of being able to say I had a collection out helped with audiences, publishers, editors, local papers, writers-on-tour schemes, etc". Publication opens doors. First books are undeniably attractive things. When should you do it? Certainly not as soon as possible. Too early in your writing career and you will live to regret it. There is nothing quite like being haunted by the dreadful, ill-formed verse of your youth in your accomplished later age. Pound admits that perhaps he had printed too much of his early poetry. A few Anglo-Welsh poets have openly disowned theirs with one or two going as far as to exclude that abominable first compilation of poetic blunder from their bibliographies. My own early titles regularly get listed but I can't tell you how glad I am that they are so difficult to actually get hold of. Those awkward stumbles pushed into print to prove I could do it actually did nothing of the sort although I never understood this at the time. Sam Adams wrote that a monkey loose on a typewriter could have done better. He was right. Gillian Clarke counsels leaving your mss in a drawer for a few years. She says 10, which may be too long, but in essence her advice is sound.

Despite such counsel most people choose to go ahead as soon as possible. Ready or not their book is going to come out, so we might as well concentrate on learning how to make the best of it. As Gertrude Stein has it "successions of words are so agreeable" — but how many successions make a book? Poetry has a long tradition of appearing as slim volumes, some of them so slim that to deem them volumes is to exaggerate in the extreme. A couple of great poetry firsts of the Twentieth Century have titles like *18 Poems* and *25 Poems* so you can see that there is often not much to an initial collection. If your average poem runs to 40 lines or less and you can assemble 25 or so with which you are reasonably pleased then you have the makings of a book. If you can manage only 10 then it is a pamphlet. You can insist on calling this a book until such time as you publish a larger assemblage whereupon you may begin the slow process of discrediting by referring to your first as a leaflet. No hard and fast rules, the choice is yours.

I would advise that whatever you do try not to throw together the first few dozen poems you have knocked out and expect them to work as a cohesive whole. Assembling a successful book requires effort. Anthony Howell succinctly explains — "Presentation, order, theme — all these are issues which count. Also your own fastidiousness — each word, each punctuation mark, each line-break should, I feel, be the result of deliberation. A 'completed' manuscript can be made far better if you tune it up for several months *after* you think you've finished it. Don't send it out, I'd say, before this tune-up is completed. This is easier said of course; in the event, you always notice a fault minutes after you've sent a copy winging its way through the post".

An important consideration for any poet ought to be how they imagine their collection is going to sell. Who will buy it? Why will they buy it? How will they get to hear about it? Where will they get their hands on a copy? All questions most writers consider the province of the publisher, but all questions which will need answering at some stage, and if the answers are not positive then the book is unlikely to appear. Contrary to popular belief there is no mass of poetry buyers out there eager to embrace every new name that comes onto the market. Libraries have limited resources; collectors into books by unknowns are rare. Who are you? Why will people want to buy your verse? In order to get a book sold the poet must help create the market. Naturally the publisher will do some work but the ground must have be prepared in advance by the author. What this means in practical terms is that you have to get your name about a bit — be published in the magazines, be known on the readings circuit, enter competitions — anything to increase awareness of your name and your talent.

Once you have put together your bag of verse, checked and re-checked for quality, style and effectiveness, you should add an arresting title. Many poets take the easy route and name their books after an included poem. *Howl and Other Poems, Barry Island and Other Poems, Putting Kingsley Amis in the Microwave.* This may work well enough but do check that another book of the same name doesn't already exist. Sally Jones' *Turning Away*, her successful first book, was almost *A Way of Looking* before she discovered that Elizabeth Jennings already had a volume out under that name.

"A good title should be like a good metaphor — it should intrigue without being too baffling or too obvious." — Walker Percy. Be original. *How Green Was My Valley* is in use. *Hamlet and Other Poems* is somewhat derivative. Steer clear of the lofty precociousness of things like *The Poetic Thoughts of Gladys Evans* — few would want to read them anyway. Recent titles which have intrigued and impressed me include Adam Thorpe's *Mornings in the Baltic,* Ken Smith's *Book of Chinese Whispers*, Paul Muldoon's *Meeting the British*, Adrian Mitchell's *On The Beach at Cambridge*, Hans Magnus Enzesberger's *The Sinking of the Titanic*, Carol Ann Duffy's *Standing Female Nude*, and perhaps the best of the lot, Bob Cobbing's *Lame Limping Mangled Marred and Mutilated* — a graphic encapsulation of the poet's methods. These titles the customer remembers. This is half the battle.

The big question for every initiate is where to send the mss once you have finished tinkering. Should you use a literary agent to help you avoid the agony of dealing with possible rejection? Probably not. Most agents are not in the least interested in poetry and unless you happen to be a best-selling novelist who also dabbles in verse you will inevitably have to place your book on your own.

The whole business of what is publishable and what is not is decided subjectively. Tastes change. The notion of what is 'good poetry' changes as time moves on. Getting a poetry book accepted is not like having litmus paper change colour as it contacts acid. There is an element of luck, a good deal of sending in to the right place at the right time, a little of who you are and who you know and yes, the quality of the work has some bearing too. There is enough to say on the technique of getting published to fill a book. Luckily you are holding it. In addition to the information which follows check out Chapter Eleven which covers mainstream publishers and Chapter Twelve which details some of Britain's smaller presses.

Poetry publishers split readily into three types.

* National Trade publishers such as Hutchinson (who publish Dannie Abse), Faber & Faber, Chatto and Windus, Oxford University Press, Jonathan Cape, and Sinclair-Stevenson. Occasionally these companies are joined by Macmillan, Virago, The Women's Press, Dent and Collins Harvill. With the possible exception of Faber the main business here is not verse but general publishing, although the owners are concerned enough with literature to find it worthwhile bringing out a number of volumes from time to time.

* Specialists like Seren (founded as Poetry Wales Press), Bloodaxe, Carcanet, Peterloo Poets, Enitharmon, Littlewood Arc, and Anvil have as their prime purpose the publishing of verse and do so in a professional and vigorous manner, usually with the aid of subsidy.

* The small and little presses — the original backbone of poetry publishing, run as hobbies (or obsessions) by literate (and illiterate) individuals up and down the country. The small presses are hundreds strong — ever changing — a mixture of amateur and professional with production standards at all levels. They often present the best hope for the newcomer. Examples include Writers Forum, Red Sharks Press, Smith/Doorstop, Rockingham Press, Stride Publications and the Hippopotamus Press.

Who should you try? Start at the top but be prepared to work your way down. Do some research. Check out the products of the poetry presses in your local bookshop. Send away for small press publications. Keep your eye on the review pages of literary periodicals. See who is being published and by whom. Send in your mss to the active publishers. Keep your ear to the ground. In a sense it is a game. Your mss may well bounce about between dozens of publishers before one takes a liking to it or you may be lucky and hit gold with your first submission. For the most part, though, books tend to come back with rejection slips attached. *The editor regrets...read with interest...not quite suitable...publishing programme full...best of luck elsewhere...thank you for sending...etc.* Do not be depressed. Robert Morgan pasted 620 similar missives into a scrapbook which he carried around with him to readings in order to prove to the aspiring that the road upwards can be deliriously tough.

Do remember to enclose sufficient return postage along with a large enough envelope with your mss when you send it off. Unsolicited mss go into a slush pile at the larger publishers and get read slowly, often by outside readers. Those without SAE are unlikely to ever come back.

Once you've got your first book accepted the sun will come out. Bask in the warmth for just a while. You have done it. Shortly the critics will be taking you to pieces and all your friends will own a copy. After this there will be a silence. You will wonder what real difference all this has made. Have you made it as a poet? No good looking backwards. To find out for sure that you have got there you must now do it again.

Where to find out more:

The Writer's Handbook, published every year by Macmillan, lists publishers of books and magazines worldwide as does *The Writers' and Artists' Yearbook* put out by A & C Black. Every self respecting serious writer should own one of these. Pretty useful as well is the address list *Small Presses and Little Magazines of the UK and Ireland* put out by Oriel bookshop with help from the Association of Little Presses. Appendix VI contains the addresses of a good many possibles. Those concerned to stay within the borders of Wales can consider the following:

Alun Books, Sally Roberts Jones, 3 Crown Street, Port Talbot. (Publishes professional looking literary and local history titles as well as the occasional poetry collection.)

The Collective, John Jones, Penlanlas Farm, Llantilo Pertholey, Y Fenni, Gwent, NP7 7HN. (Co-operative small scale poetry pamphlet publishing, an outgrowth of the twice monthly writers group meeting at The Hill in Abergavenny.)

Envoi Poets Press, Anne Lewis-Smith, Pen Ffordd, Newport, Dyfed, SA42 OQT. (The booklet publishing section of *Envoi* magazine, now run by Roger Elkin from Stoke-on-Trent. Concentrates on small first editions by new poets generally subsidised by the writer concerned.)

Gwasg Gomer/The Gomer Press, Llandysul, Dyfed, SA44 4BQ. (Publishing arm of J.D.Lewis and Sons, Wales's principal Welsh language publisher. Produces a large number of Welsh interest books annually including a small selection of subsidised English language poetry titles.)

Headland Publications, Tŷ Coch, Galltegfa, Llanfwrog, Ruthin, Clwyd, LL15 2AR. (The Welsh address of Gladys Mary Coles' Merseyside based poetry operation. Produces at least one professional if marginally old fashioned looking pamphlet annually.)

Honno, Ailsa Craig, Heol y Cawl, Dinas Powys, South Glamorgan, CF6 4AH. (The Welsh women's press run by a co-operative. Produces a small number of exciting and professional looking books annually. Includes titles by individual women as well as thematic poetry anthologies.)

Llanerch Publishers, Felinfach, Lampeter, Dyfed, SA48 8PJ. (Desk top originated small press style histories and facsimile reprints of

classics in the main but has dabbled with original verse — Steve
Short's new *Gododdin* re-work for example.)

Lolfa, Talybont, Dyfed, SY24 5HE. (Mainly Welsh language editions
including a series of 'unofficial' poets. Occasionally publishes
English language poetry of specific Welsh interest.)

Red Sharks Press, operator Christopher Mills, 122 Clive Street,
Grangetown, Cardiff, CF1 7JE. (Classic one man little press concentrating on poetry and short fiction in handbuilt but snappy
looking small editions.)

Seren, poetry editor Amy Wack, First Floor, 2 Wyndham Street,
Bridgend, Mid Glamorgan, CF31 1EF. (Specialist and highly professional literary pubilisher with national UK distribution. Puts
out around 6 poetry titles per year mostly by Welsh poets writing
in English.)

Swansea Poetry Workshop, 124 Overland Road, Mumbles, Swansea,
SA3 4EU. (The J.C. Evans, Nigel Jenkins and Malcolm Parr occasional co-operative publisher. Despite its title not interested in
new mss.)

In addition Wales boasts a number of very small presses now either
relatively inactive or devoted mainly to the work of their operators.
These include Underground Press (John Evans, 9 Lanelay Tce, Mae-
sycoed, Pontypridd, Mid Glamorgan), Cwm Nedd Press (Robert
King, 16 Rhydhir, Neath Abbey, Neath, West Glamorgan), Kerrin
Publishers (Irene & Keith Thomas, 29 Glan yr Afon, Ebbw Vale,
Gwent, NP3 5NR), Spareman Press (Joe Pumford, 65 Sycamore
Avenue, Newport, Gwent, NP9 9AJ), Chiron Press (9 Hamilton
Street, Cardiff), Rebec Press (79 Bronwydd Road, Carmarthen,
Dyfed, SA31 2AP), Zena (Croesor, Gwynedd, LL48 6SR) and Swan
Books (E.O. Evans, 13 Henrietta Street, Swansea SA1 4HW). Two
commercial publishers based in Wales, The University of Wales Press
(Gwennyth Street, Cathays, Cardiff) and Christopher Davies Ltd (PO
Box 403, Sketty, Swansea, SA2 9BE) both publish literary works and
have occasionally brought out poetry titles. There are also two highly
regarded private presses publishing limited edition works in special-
ist bindings, the Old Style Press (Frances & Nicholas McDowell,
Catchmays Court, Llandogo, Nr Monmouth, Gwent, NP5 4TN) and
Gwasg Gregynog (Newtown, Powys, SY16 3PW). Paul Peter Piech's
Taurus Press Of Willow Dene, run from 11 Limetree Way, Danygraig,

Porthcawl, Mid Glamorgan, CF36 5AU, publishes not books but poetry posters, all illustrated with the owner's inimitable wood cuts.

A fuller survey of mainstream UK publishers of poetry will be found in Chapter Eleven. UK small presses are covered in Chapter Twelve.

Chapter Six

Why Do You Publish — Ego Or Art?
The Vanity Presses

People tend to get very upset about the Vanity Presses. They are the poetry world's classic swindle. The system is about as direct as it can be. Money for fame. It works like this: vanity operators place small ads in the classifieds of the Sunday papers and in the personal columns of wide circulation weekly magazines. We've all seen these things:

> POEMS WANTED. Publisher seeks new authors. Send your verse now to Dept PW23...

> PUBLISHER WITH EXPANDING LIST SEEKS POETRY. Send with SAE to...

> POETS does your work deserve publication? Contributions sought for exciting new anthology *Golden Gems Of The British Muse — Poems To Treasure*. Send with SAE to Department Z...

And those of us who have any knowledge of the poetry business at all will know that no publisher ever need actually advertise for material. Even the barest indication that someone might be into publishing poetry usually results in them being deluged with un-called for mss. Advertisements for poetry should be treated with suspicion from the start.

The unsuspecting however respond with glee and after the passage of a day or so receive a glowing letter in return:

> *We thank you for submitting your work and are pleased to tell you that our editor is most impressed with your obvious talent. Accordingly we are accepting your poems 'The Love Song of Alfred J Perkins' and 'The Bells of Barry Island' for inclusion in our forthcoming anthology* New Lyrics of Huge Importance. *This splendid publication is held in high regard by those in the poetry world and is regarded as an arbiter of taste for succeeding generations of writers. It circulates among the editors of most national newspapers including the Daily Mirror, Daily Express*

and the Daily Mail and can be found on the shelves of the National Library of Scotland, The National Library of Wales, The Bodleian Library Oxford, The Library of Cambridge University, The Library of Trinity College Dublin and the British Library, London.

The inclusion of one or more examples of your first class writing will undoubtedly enhance the volume considerably. Poets of real ability are all too rare.

The effect of such a letter on the uncertain, unpublished should not be underestimated. Unsuspecting teetotallers suddenly informed of their obvious talent have been known to stand rounds. Self-conscious wallflowers brought face to face with their real ability have danced on tables.

The letter proceeds to detail the many "necessary legal clauses" of the publishing arrangement between poet and press. It continues at length about subsidiary rights, reprint considerations, proof of ownership, etc, finally culminating in a short paragraph reading something like:

In order to help the publisher defray rising printing costs at this time we are asking you for a small contribution of £50 per poem. Please make your cheques payable to the Georgian Press and send as soon as possible to...

It is the sting but the uninitiated never notice. Obvious talent is paramount. They send the cheque off without a murmur.

What is happening here is that poets are paying to have their poems included in a duff anthology which will be read by no one but the contributors themselves. It will be a poorly printed volume with poems jammed in like adverts for second hand cars. The libraries mentioned so importantly in the initial letter are the UK's copyright receipt repositories and by law receive every book produced in this country. The newspapers listed do not review poetry. Bookshops and literary journals know the Vanity Presses for what they are and ignore their products. There has been no value judgement at any stage. What then is any of this worth?

It is probable that these direct attempts to trick money out of the less aware writer are less prevalent today than they once were. In the 60s vanity presses were an epidemic. Their products were so undesirable and so unsaleable that I once came upon a whole builders skip full of *Diadems of the British Muse 1969*, valueless even as pulp. I still have the one or two copies I rescued as examples of what to avoid. Among the 100 or so contributors I recognise not one name. Poetry even had its own version of the Guardian Angels in the form of *Poet's Vigilantes* — an organisation set up to rescue the unwary.

Writers are generally unwilling to acknowledge having been caught like this. I surveyed a few dozen before writing this article and only one — Jacob Bush — was willing to admit to any involvement. My own early, and dreadfully juvenile poems were regularly published in what I took to be a genuine magazine, *Poet's Platform*. This was a duplicated, 'jam them in three columns to the page' job, but how was I to know that this was not how it should be done. The mag was actually a front for an innovative vanity operation. After a number of successfully published contributions I received the come-on letter telling me that my wonderful work had been selected for broadcast by radio stations across the world and would I meet the publishers at the Park Hotel, Cardiff. A small note told me that if I was under 21 to bring an adult along. I took my mother. The interview was held in a plushly carpeted room filled with huge speakers and conducted by a glamorous South African woman. My poetry, she informed us, was so terrific that they had set it to music. The world market was out there trembling with bates in its breath. We were then treated to a recitation of my masterpiece, "Pounding Sound", read by a deep-voiced actor to a background of slushy strings. I was stunned. This was me, my words, my own creation. I had arrived. My mother was almost in tears with the joy of it all. "This is great material," the South African told us, "it will make you a fortune." All we had to do, apparently, was to find the several hundred pounds needed to produce 'studio quality' recordings and the company would then do the rest. We went away and considered the matter and naturally found the cash. There was a chance for me to be famous and make money. I was going to take it. As the months passed *Poet's Platform* remained strangely silent. No royalty cheques reached our door. Sightly worried I wrote the company a letter asking how things were going. It was returned marked 'gone away'. We never heard from them again. And what was my poem like, viewed now from the perspective of twenty-five years? Terrible. And the world radio market for such things? Doesn't exist, never did.

To be caught, of course, poets have to a certain degree to be gullible. It is a quirk of the poetry business that people with no experience, no practice and certainly no knowledge of the world of verse imagine themselves to be struck with sufficient God-sent inspiration to produce overnight masterpieces. It is like spotting a tidy bentwood coat-rack at a friend's and thinking you'll knock one up on the kitchen table when you get home. The vanity presses feed on this. Send them any kind of garbage and they'll accept it. It has been done — cut-ups, bits of newspaper, celebrated poems of the famous, jottings of a four- year-old — they've all been accepted with the same swift praise. As long as £50 is attached anything goes.

But the tricks do not stop there. Once poets are proved to be willing to support their writing with cash new methods will be devised to part them from their money with even greater speed. Edward Uhlan, the self-confessed 'rogue of publishers' row' admits in his autobiography "at one time I ran six different poetry enterprises out of one building, each under a different editorial pseudonym". His approach was to set up a stream of poetry competitions offering real but low value prizes and to follow these up with a letter to the failed entrants offering to print their poems in a forthcoming anthology — so long, naturally, as they paid.

> In such a matter ethics and honesty are synonymous: people were willing to pay me for a specified service, and if I performed that service to their satisfaction the profits I made were certainly ethical — and deserved.
> — Edward Uhlan *The Rogue Of Publisher's Row. (Exposition Banner)*.

It is a point of view. What Uhlan fails to mention is that most of the people availing themselves of his service were, through ignorance, in no position to judge its worth.

A variation on the vanity theme is subsidy publishing. This is a fraudster's paradise too. The practise of authors assisting their publishers with the costs of publishing is as old as printing itself. But for Uhlan and his kind a share in the venture is not enough. They want the lot. The poets get their books, certainly. But not cheaply, not well produced, not well designed, not marketed, not distributed. The poets, inexperienced in the ways of the booktrade, are saddled with hundreds (if not thousands) of copies and are expected to dispose of them themselves. Not always easy. Worse the subsidy publisher will encourage its prey to pay extra for a number of outrageously expensive and completely unfashionable additions to the edition such as their name gold-blocked onto the cover, having the binding done in yak-hide and the thing printed on paper woven underwater by virgins in the Ecuador. Gregynog Press look out.

Expose these swine, people ask. Print a list of their names. But the moment you do this they change their names, start up somewhere else. It's like duff double glazing. If you are really worried check with The Society of Authors (84 Drayton Gardens, London, SW10 9SB. Tel: 071 373 6642), The Poetry Society (22 Betterton Street, London, WC2H 9BU. Tel: 071 240 4810) or The Poetry Library, (Royal Festival Hall, London, SE1 8XX. Tel: 071 921 0943).

One step down from the clear-cut subsidy swindlers are the ubiquitous small presses who produce hundreds of different pamphlets by countless poets, none of which ever seem to be on sale in any of the specialist outlets and few of which are ever heard of again. These dubious operations, often run in tandem with apparently genuine literary magazines, increase their grip on the unsuspecting poet by stealth. You submit your work and it is accepted. Later you are invited to contribute to the magazine's pamphlet series. Small stuff compared with mainline subsidy publishing but you are still obliged to pay. The borderline between exploitation and genuine small press publisher/author co-production is a fine one. A case which exemplifies just how fine is that of the late Howard Sergeant MBE, founder and editor of *Outposts*, one of the UK 's longest running magazines. Sergeant was a respected editor and servant of poetry. He had been awarded his MBE for his services to literature and was a fine poet in his own right, but he had a penchant for bringing out pamphlets by complete unknowns in exchange for money. The idea had started well enough. Early Outposts booklets included first titles by the likes of Alan Sillitoe, Kevin Crossley Holland, Peter Reading and Harry Guest. But as time passed the pull of profit began to cloud Sergeant's judgement. Less accomplished writers joined the throng in increasing numbers, eventually leading to Outposts becoming the UK's largest poetry publisher, in terms of number of titles if not turnover. The catch was, as ever, that the authors had to pay well for and market their books themselves. On publication they received the entire print run. It is worth noting that the present *Outposts* magazine under editor Roland John is an entirely different set up. The less accomplished continue to be exploited — but elsewhere.

There are any number of dubious establishments in operation on the fringes of the poetry scene. Their operators seem to be engaged in almost everything from offering enormously expensive critical advice to running competitions with extremely low first prizes. There are the song sharks who, in exchange for an exorbitant fee, offer to set your poems to music: "Songwriters — Tin Pan Alley is looking for new hit writers". So it is — but having a few tuneless piano chords plonked behind your poems is not going to allow you to join them.

Beware too of magazines which will not have anything to do with you unless you 'join'. This usually means paying well over the odds for the privilege of submitting your stuff. A periodic rip-off are the *Who's Who Directory Of Poets* which in addition to entries on a few names — Hughes, Redgrove, Causley, et al consist mainly — 90% even — of entries on Mrs X, hobbies gardening and cats, 2 poems in *Diadem of the British Muse* last year. Alexis Lykiard reminds me that in the 70s a librarian took one such publisher to court under the Trades Descriptions Act and won damages. The directory could not possibly be considered a realistic who's who. The rake off for the publisher was to get those included to buy copies of the finished directories together with a framed certificate testifying to their inclusion, or perhaps a leather slip case with name blocked on in gold leaf and a snake-skin bookmark forever marking the poet's place.

How many other methods are there? In America the bogus sounding *World of Poetry's* Board of Directors are handing out Golden Poet Awards — "the highest honor World of Poetry ever bestows on a poet". Completely free too — only you have to pay about 500 golden dollars for registration at the three day convention where these amazing bits of yellow, ductile paper get presented. Not available in Britain yet but no doubt coming soon. I sometimes get the feeling that this whole totteringly amateur business is ninety per cent charlatan. Anyone with an interest in the work of others must be a con-artist. But it really isn't like that. Most of the poetry world is surprisingly genuine. Publishers, editors and organisers often work long hours for nothing more than the pleasure of seeing what they believe in encouraged. But watch for the sharks. Write for writing's sake. It is this fame business that enables them to bite.

Chapter Seven

Doing It Yourself

This is the worst day of my life. My manuscript has been returned.
— Eric Lane

It's an awful business. For some of us there seems to be a kind of inevitability about our failure to get a book out. The reasons can be many: wrong poems, bad poems, inability, inefficiency, wrong time, wrong publisher, bloody mindedness, even that old favourite — a conspiracy to keep you out. The results are always the same. Darkness and depression as we feed our life's work slowly into the flames.

A way out which many have taken is to avoid the sordid business of dealing with publishers altogether. Go it alone — publish yourself. If you can put up a shelf then there is a fair chance you will be able to make the book to go on it as well. However, there are a few psychological problems with which to be contended first. Writers think that:

* Self-publication is an act of vanity and somehow dishonourable
* It cannot possibly be as good as the real thing
* Proper writers don't do it.

Actually they are wrong on three counts, especially the third. There is nothing vain or even vaguely dishonourable about wanting to see your work printed. And it can be as good as the real thing, of course, — it is simply a matter of knowing how. As to proper writers not doing it — the reality is that an amazing number of pretty eminent literary figures have at some time during their careers had a hand in bringing out a book themselves. Edgar Allen Poe, D.H. Lawrence, Ezra Pound, James Joyce, Virginia Woolf, Anaïs Nin. Rumour has it that Eliot started out by financing *Prufrock and Other Observations* from his own pocket but he didn't. Pound raised the cash for him. Not quite the same. However, R.S. Thomas did pay for the Druid Press to bring out his first book and then had to help the Montgomeryshire Press with the distribution of *An Acre Of Land*, his second. Getting ink on your sleeves in the pursuit of publication is not as uncommon as many imagine.

William Carlos Williams' first book *Poems* which appeared in 1909 was a typical case of the unpublished trying to solve the problem by self-intervention. Williams took his work to a neighbourhood jobbing printer who agreed to do the work for $50.

> The local journeymen, never having set up anything like it in their lives, must have been completely baffled. When I saw the first copy I nearly fainted. It was full of errors. I still have it, with Pop's corrections all through it and suggestions for changes, most of which I adopted. I took a dozen or so of the revised pamphlet to the local stationery store. The price was 25c. About four copies were sold. I gave others away. Mr Howell (the printer) wrapped up the remainder for safekeeping, about a hundred copies. They were inadvertently burned ten years later.
> — Willam Carlos Williams *I Wanted To Write A Poem*, New Directions, 1978.

The Anglo-Welsh as a breed on the other hand have not been great self-publishers. Opportunities for the promulgation of collections in Wales have generally been good. However there are always reasons for bypassing the established system. Tony Curtis brought out *Out Of The Dark Wood* under his *Edge Press* imprint as a quick way of putting an introduction of his work onto the market. John Idris Jones self-published both his *Way Back To Ruthin* and *Barry Island And Other Poems* because he was rightly convinced he could do things better than regular publishers. Duncan Bush did his *Red Mouths, Black Faces* for reasons of expediency at the time of the miner's strike. A few others have dabbled: Christopher Mills, Labi Siffre, Nigel Jenkins, Janet Dube, John Freeman, Childe Roland — mostly writers on the fringes of the mainstream who have either regarded publication by the established companies as a form of compromise or prefer to keep all the financial returns, such as they may be, for themselves.

How Big?

If you do decide to bring yourself out, because you are publishing against the grain, because you want a book out now not next year or even simply because no one else seems interested in your work, how big an undertaking will it be? If books are icebergs then the writing is the part you see above water. Publishing and selling are the dark enormities sailing underneath. It is wise not to underestimate this aspect of book production. Publication requires as much if not more effort than the act of writing in the first place. Anyone with a few hundred pounds to spare and a bunch of 20 or 30 poems can turn up at the local printers and arrange for a book of sorts to be run off. Many do this and the results are nearly always the same. A dull, lifeless lump of a product which doesn't sell and which no one wants to read. How on earth can anyone get excited about a plain unillustrated 30 pager called *The Poetic Thoughts Of Beryl Coombs?* When you pick it up the pages start to come loose. When you try to read them you find the ink faded. If you manage a line or two you discover them to be mis-spelled. Too many self-publications end up looking like this.

The solution is careful planning. Match your resources to your ability. Do not rush. Read up on the subject. The following will give you a good start:

How To Publish Yourself — Peter Finch, Allison and Busby.
Publishing Your Own Book — Jon Wynne-Tyson, Centaur Press.
Publishing & Printing At Home — Roy Lewis and John B. Easson, David & Charles.
Guide To Self-Publishing — Harry Mulholland, Mulholland Wirral.
Publish It Yourself & Make It Pay — Ian Templeton, Pikers Pad.
The Writer's Guide To Self Publishing — Charlie Bell, Dragonfly Press.
Into Print — *How to Make Desktop Publishing Work For You* —- Susan Quilliam & Ian Grove-Stephensen, BBC Books.
How To Publish A Book — Robert Spicer, How To Books.

Buy a copy or try your local library. If they haven't a copy insist they get one.

How Much?

A lot depends on how big a book you want, how well you expect it to be printed and how many copies you want. An average first pamphlet could well be 30 poems, set on a word processor, and run off on a photocopier with a printer-produced card cover in an edition of 250. With a bit of hunting around such things could be done for between £150 and £200. This is not the only way to do it, of course, but it is an inexpensive first approach.

What Next

Unfortunately for those of a retiring nature publishing does not stop once the book rolls in from the printer. At least half the task remains still to be done. Marketing, a term familiar to multinational conglomerates, must be considered by self-publishers as well. By the time your completed book first reaches you it should be appropriately titled, reasonably priced, and attractively produced — all things which will give it a fair chance of getting noticed. This is not at all impossible to achieve. Most poets can do it. The problem is that a lot don't.

Sod's Law

If it is possible to foul it up, your average self-publishing poet will. Through inexperience books appear in editions of 10,000 with titles mis-spelled, contact addresses missing and the poems bound in upside down. Pricing will end up ludicrously inappropriate with little thought ever having been given to everyday overheads like postage, packing and booksellers discounts. Promotion will be nil. The existence of the book will be kept a total secret from everyone except the local newspaper which will print a photograph of the author holding a copy of his or her new book under the banner of "Local Bard hits the Big Time" but will fail to name the title and will be totally reticent about where copies can be had. Such books will not fit into any standard envelope known to stationers, nor will they fit onto bookshop shelves. If they have a spine it will have nothing printed on it. When you pick it up and gingerly turn to the contents the pages will fall out.

Such production jobs are not limited to self-published poets either. Probably the biggest single category of offenders in the book publishing business is local government, who through years of connection with the local library service ought to know better, but do not.

How To Win

To do things correctly is to give yourself a chance. It is not difficult.

Plan the book right through to the last detail — title, pages, contents, text, the lot. Construct a mock-up. Find an attractive book by someone else and copy it.

Work out how many you can sell. Poetry does not go like hot cakes — most book buyers will run miles before opening such a volume. Do you know 100 people? Will they relieve you of copies? How many will you give away? Don't forget to send out liberal quantities of review copies to all and sundry.

Confirm your printing method. Self done on typewriter and photocopier, desk top published (which for the uninitiated means sophisticated origination on a home computer and then run by a local print shop) or fully set and litho printed down the road. Who will bind the pages? What about overall design and illustration for the front cover? These are not down to the printer who will merely do as asked. You must decide.

Calculate your retail price. Multiply your unit production cost by at least three which should allow you enough for booksellers' 33% discount and basic overheads like postage.

Get an ISBN allocated. Think about using a barcode. Bone up on copyright information so you get the text for the verso (back) of the title page correct.

Give your enterprise a name. *The Mike Jenkins Publishing Company* is not good enough. Try *Heol Gerrig Books* instead. "Hello, this is *Gerrig Books* here. We've just taken on this cracking new author called Mike Jenkins and have a book of his due out next week. How many copies would you like?"

Send review copies everywhere: local papers, media, poetry magazines, literary journals — do not begrudge them as freebies. They are your ticket to success.

Tackle the bookstores. Write to friends and relatives. Visit poetry readings with an armful of copies. Make a nuisance of yourself. Best of luck.

Organisations which may help:

Association of Little Presses, the long-lived original small press and little magazine support group. Membership costs a mere £10 for which you get a regular newsletter of printing tips and small publishing information, a subsciption to Palpi "Poetry and Little Press Information" magazine, copies of the Association's annual *Catalogue of Little Press Books In Print* replete with news and information from the small publishing, self-publishing and poetry scene, plus the chance to participate in the many ALP bookfairs and exhibitions up and down the country. The ALP is open to all manner of publishers but does have a bias towards poetry and creative writing. Write to 89a Petherton Road, London, N5 2QT. Tel: 071 226 2657.

The Author-Publisher Enterprise, a genuine self-publishers' group founded by swimming pool expert John Dawes. The group publish an excellent newsletter containing hard-edged information and advice — *Write To Publish* — and run regular group meetings, seminars and road shows. Write to the Secretary, Trevor Lockwood, PO Box 1844, Colchester, Essex, CO3 3SL. Tel: 0206 752778.

The Small Press Group, Britain's largest organisation of small presses, autonomous publishers and independent magazines. Similar to the ALP, membership here costs £17.50 for which you get a subscription to the magazine *Small Press World*, regular newsletters, copies of the annual *SPG Yearbook* which is literally packed with information, contact addresses and tips for small and self-publishers, representation at the many SPG bookfairs and use of the recently formed Small Press Centre where the SPG is now based. Write to them c/o Middlesex University, White Hart Lane, London, N17 3HR.

Companies Offering Short Run Printing And Assistance for Self-Publishers:

Antony Rowe Ltd, Bumper's Farm, Chippenham, Wiltshire, SN14 6QA. Tel: 0249 659705.

Catford Copy Centre, P0 Box 563, Catford, London SE6 4PY. Tel: 081 695 0101.

Intype, Woodman Works, Durnsford Road, Wimbledon, London, SW19 8DR. Tel: 081 947 7863.

DOING IT YOURSELF

Laserbacks, Ann Kritzinger Ltd, 20 Shepherds Hill, London, N6
   5AH. Tel: 081 341 7650.
Words & Images, 2 Charlton Cottages, Barden Road, Speldhurst,
   Tunbridge Wells, Kent, TN3 0LH. Tel: 0892 862395.

In Wales an unrivalled complete service from free initial advice on
concept and design to the finished product is available from:

Keith James Design, 39 Charles Street, Cardiff, CF1 4EB. Tel: 0222
   222117.

Chapter Eight

The Literary Magazine — A Round-Up Of The Main Operators

People don't buy literary magazines much. Looking at displays of tidily produced and well-designed issues of *Planet, Poetry Wales* and *The New Welsh Review* I get the impression that this is an attempt at selling to the mass market, working the same field as perhaps *Woman, Q,* or *Radio Times,* or even those huge circulation throwaways from the eighties *Prima, Bella,* and *Best.* Style, gloss and slickness are the marks. But commercial success does not come from appearance alone. Literary magazines circulate among a select group — *Poetry Wales,* 800 copies; *Prima,* three-quarters of a million. Some gap.

Why don't more people buy literary littles? No one is really sure. It is not for want of advertising and promotion campaigns on behalf of the publishers, that's for certain. Top whack seems to be the unbreachable 5000 copies achieved by the likes of *Poetry Review* and *Stand.* Beyond that sales will not go.

There have been attempts to manufacture something that will. All-purpose writers' mags which try to tap into the UK-wide network of writer's circles; national distributor backed semi-glossies, hefty top-line poet doorstops, tabloid format cheapies — all of them failures. It is as if the market for new creative literature just is not there. The circulation of most magazines turns out to be so small that it can only ever be read by its contributors, friends of its contributors, potential contributors plus a few academics who would like to be contributors but for various reasons are not. Library copies, file copies, copyright copies and review freebies which can on occasion account for as much as half of some magazine's total printing drop into a black hole from which most never emerge. Poetry mags serve no ready market. They are there for the writer's sake alone.

There are a lot of them too. 2000 worldwide in Len Fulton's *Directory of Poetry Publishers,* over 300 in Oriel's *Small Presses and*

Little Magazines of the UK, An Address List. The diversification is endless. As an exercise Fulton surveyed his 2000 entrants asking them to nominate five poets they had published recently. No Ted Hughes or John Ashbery up top. Instead at No 1: Lyn Lifshin, No 2: William Stafford, No 3: Arthur W. Knight. Allen Ginsberg got in at No 7 while way down the list at No 11, just after B.Z. Niditch, was Seamus Heaney. Reputation may help in order to get you published but it's certainly no prerequisite. Who is this Niditch anyway?

In the UK magazines can be split into three types. First is the larger, well produced and often subsidised journal with aspirations to represent the best of current writing nationwide. Second the more specialized mag often with access to financial help of some sort which carries the work of a specific region, group or literary specialisation. Third the general, enthusiastically put together magazine of writing for writing's sake — all contributions welcome — the classic little. Any attempt to survey these rather arbitrary groupings is bound to run into difficulty. Comprehensiveness is out on grounds of numbers, and things change fast too. Review it and the next you hear is that it has gone out of business. Therefore the belt around the poetry bazaar I present covers only those magazines I have seen in recent times. Do not regard it as definitive, but as an outline map it won't be too bad. For addresses check Appendix V.

Way out front in representing poetry in English from this side of the Atlantic is *PN Review* (sample copy — £4.00). Founded in 1973 as a sort of Carcanet Press house magazine it has now become a nationally distributed A4 format soft-front in the style of *The New Statesman and Society* or *Barn*. It is published 6 times a year and edited by Michael Schmidt, co-ordinated by Ronald Decent and put into place with the assistance of a high powered team of contributing editors including Gabriel Josipovici, John Pilling, Stuart Hood and Nicolas Tredell. *PN Review* takes itself and its subject very seriously. It goes in for the literary essay, the discursive review, the in-depth study of Raymond Williams, of Yves Bonnefoy and Donald Davie, articles on the literary connections of Christianity, on the lyric in contemporary poetry, on the scene in Trieste, in St Petersburg, as well as running translations from European languages and interviews with the cultural thinkers of our time. The poetry it uses is well turned and authoritative although rarely rip-roaringly exciting. Recent numbers have included C.H. Sisson, F.T. Prince, Les Murray, Iain Crichton Smith, Ruth Fainlight, D.J. Enright and John Heath-Stubbs.

THE LITERARY MAGAZINE

PN Review gives us a lot to read. Subtitled "poems, essays, fiction, reviews, interviews, comment" it represents mainstream English literary intellectualism of a very high standard. This of course means that it is no arena for the amateur, has little space for poetry's radical edges and no room at all for textual experiments. No matter how magazines may attempt it they cannot be all things to all people. Under Schmidt and his team the *PN Review* doesn't even try.

A magazine of a totally different complexion and founded a lot earlier, in 1959, is *Ambit* — a quarto-sized spine-bound journal of poetry and new fiction enlivened with a large helping of contemporary art work. Editor is Martin Bax, backed up with a luminous team of assistants and corresponding editors including Edwin Brock, Carol Ann Duffy, J.G. Ballard, E.A. Markham, Eduardo Paolozzi, Anselm Hollo and Henry Graham. The sort of work *Ambit* uses is way off centre. It is hardly amateur little mag stuff but neither is it drawn from the Larkin-Abse-Motion extended Movement tradition. Bax has a penchant for 60s and 70s radicalism eschewing the language orientated experimenting of the 80s and not being all that keen on European innovations either. Nonetheless he likes to keep it fresh. You get a lot of new names in *Ambit* along with the more familiar: Martin Stannard, Aidan Higgins, Adrian Henri, Gavin Ewart, Carol Satyamurti, Anthony Howell, Peter Porter, Jim Burns, Paul Groves. Its fiction is readable modernist, its use of contemporary artists extensive. Its poetry book reviews are comprehensive and informative more than critical. This is no analytical platform — essays don't get a look in. As a magazine I like it a lot for its deliberate rejection of both fad and academia. More people should try it (sample copy — £5.00).

Agenda, also founded in 1959, exudes venerable authority. A pocket sized, spine-bound paperback quarterly it is one of the few British magazines around which still looks as if it were produced by letterpress. This gives it an old fashioned feel which is enhanced somewhat by its rather predictable content. Editors Peter Dale and William Cookson seek poetry showing "more than usual emotion, more than usual order", to quote Coleridge, and go in for special issues devoted to the work of twentieth century greats such as T.S. Eliot, Ezra Pound, Seamus Heaney, Tom Scott and, a particular favourite, David Jones. Their general issues print traditional-style poetry of a high standard, usually from the close circle of writers which includes Kathleen Raine, Anne Beresford, Alan Brownjohn,

W.S. Milne, Michael Hamburger, C.H. Sisson, Geoffrey Hill and William Bedford. No amateurs, no cultural foreigners, few new voices. Reliable verse with its tie on. At least half of each issue is given over to reviews. The magazine's interests are extended by the work of *Agenda Editions* which has published much sought after titles from, among others, Alan Massey, William Bedford, Anne Beresford and David Jones. (Sample copy — £4.00.)

The longest lived British literary magazine is *The Poetry Review*, founded in 1909 as the journal of the Poetry Society, but now an open and supposedly broadbased quarterly with a circulation of 5000. As might be imagined the magazine has gone through many changes in its long history. In the last twenty years it has turned from an outgoing contemporary reference point under the controversial Eric Mottram to a journal which seems fuller of reviews and articles than it does of verse, under present editor Peter Forbes. The refreshingly entertaining format introduced by previous editor Mick Imlah — filling the pages with competitions, quips, reviews of readings, gossip and literary asides — has been maintained and expanded by the present incumbent. The periodic regional round-ups, focusing on poetry activity in a specific district, have been extended to include in-depth features on specific magazines and supplemented with features on literary institutions such as The Arts Council and The Poetry Book Society — but some of the more innovative features like the infamous British and Irish Poetry Rankings seem to have been dropped. This latter piece of impertinence split poets into four hierarchical divisions, like football teams. Top of Division One is Seamus quickly followed by Ted and then Geoffrey Hill, Tony Harrison and Derek Mahon. The Welsh turn out to be better represented than might be imagined. R.S. Thomas at no 29 (Division Two), Dannie Abse at 46, Robert Minhinnick at 59, Tony Curtis at 64, Gillian Clarke at 68 (Division Three), and Oliver Reynolds at 76 (Division Four).

The kind of poetry featured by Forbes is mainstream movement although the magazine's penchant for special subject issues gives a fair amount of scope for work by outsiders. Recent numbers have focused on "The New Generation Poets", "Poetry From The Indian Subcontinent", "New British Poets", "Going Critical", "Poetry And Song", "Poetry & Science", and "New Maps Of The Poetry World". Typical contributors include Selima Hill, Anne Stevenson, Kevin Crossley-Holland, Philip Gross, Carol Rumens, Peter Redgrove,

Carol Ann Duffy, Helen Dunmore, Tony Harrison, David Constantine and Penelope Shuttle. The viewpoint is pretty centralist, the standard is consistent, the style unlikely to offend. By no means as intolerant a magazine as some may like to think. (Sample copy — £5.00.)

Approaching the subject from yet another angle is *Outposts* which, under the late Howard Sergeant, who founded it in 1944, was claiming to receive upwards of 83,000 poems per year. Not bad for an independent 40 pager. The secret was Sergeant's special effort to feature the new and the unestablished. Many great writers may have started their published careers in his pages — Seamus Heaney, Dannie Abse, Douglas Dunn, Kingsley Amis, Alan Sillitoe among them — but the bulk was and still is the classic little mag poet: warts, stumbles and flashes of glory. Towards the end of his life Sergeant began to dabble in vanity press scams, turning his magazine into a hook for the unwary who would later be sold a whole book to themselves in the *Outposts* pamphlet series (see Chapter Six). Luckily the editor who took the magazine on following Sergeant's death comes from a more upright small press background. Roland John, founder and owner of the *Hippopotamus Press*, wants to put *Outposts* back on top as a vehicle for the unrecognised in the company of the well known. Its pages are almost entirely devoted to new poetry and, allowing for John's bias towards work in translation, attempts a pretty fair coverage of the work produced in provincial circles up and down the country. The literary mafia appear to be totally absent. A typical 100 page issue will run a set of contemporary translations of the likes of Louis Aragon, Rilke, Heine, Catullus and Sappho and then follow with single poems from a wide range of writers only a few of whose names mean anything to me at all. Fred Beake, Oliver Comins, A.J. Green, Ian Mortimer, Margaret Toms, Gwyneth Hughes and Julian Stannard are typical. In addition there are special issues, recently on Derek Walcott and on Norman MacCaig, but never to the exclusion of regular contributors. Circulation is around 1500 subscribers plus bookshop sales and Roland John reads at least 50,000 potential contributions annually. (Sample copy — £3.50.)

Orbis, proudly bannering itself 'an international quarterly of poetry and prose published and edited independently by Mike Shields' is what most people imagine a classic little mag to be. A long-lived, solid read, professionally printed between glossy A5 covers, exuding enthusiasm for its subject. Mike Shields has no room for literary fashions, cliquish posturing, nor the politics of big name publishing. *Orbis* is a small poet's little mag, full of the yet to be recognised and in some cases the never to make it, but all producers of worthy work just the same. There is a hankering after lost golden ages here, evidenced in an emphasis on rhymed, strictly structured work although this is by no means the only criterion for inclusion. Shields goes in for long, chatty editorials, runs features on past masters, readers' letters and rhyme revival competitions, prints extensive notes on the small time doings of the national poetry scene, covers little mag publishing in detail, reviews the poetry output of the small presses, as well as managing to give over considerable space to poetry itself, with contributors labelled by place of residence and most, but not all of them, newish writers to boot. Don't expect literature's cutting edge. This is unashamedly little England. Typical contributors include Will Daunt, Martin Reed, Mary Sheepshanks, Diana Mann, D.J. Lightfoot, Teresa Mostyn and Sue Stewart. (Sample copy — £3.95.)

Two further journals with large circulations ought to get a look in here. Both *London Magazine* and *Stand* use a lot of poetry, but this is not their only purpose. I can imagine both continuing to sell quite well if poetry ceased to exist tomorrow. *London Magazine* is an Arts Council subsidized bi-monthly looking a little like *Reader's Digest.* Under editor Alan Ross it covers the whole arts scene from architecture to theatre, from cinema to painting. It runs a reasonable amount of fiction interspersed with new poetry. Typical contributors include Stephen Spender, Gavin Ewart, and Matthew Sweeney. Mainstream worthies all (sample copy - £5.99).

Stand, founded in 1952 and edited by the poet Jon Silkin, leans left of centre and is one of the few magazines around to present with equal weight writing from both Britain and America. *Stand's* forté is the short story, helped by having Lorna Tracy as assistant editor. Poetry, nonetheless, still plays a big part. Silkin founded the magazine as a "stand against apathy, towards new writing". It has a strong interest in the quality of the work regardless of the name on the manuscript, and strongly features foreign writers in English translation. Perhaps a little long in the tooth now to be regarded as a stamping ground for the frantically new, it is still an exciting read. Recent poets have included Medbh McGuckian, Alison Brackenbury, Michael Foley, Judith Kazantzis, and Rodney Pybus. (Sample copy— £2.50.)

There are a couple of other periodicals with some claim for inclusion in this group of top UK poetry outlets. A good one is *The Rialto*, an all poetry A4 edited by John Wakeman and Michael Mackmin, which has been steadily improving now for the past eight years. *The Rialto*, with its Norfolk arts college connections, presents an eclectic mix of high quality verse in short snatches, one or two poems per poet maximum. The feel is very much Britain in the nineties. Typical poets include Susan Wicks, Ken Smith, Glen Cavaliero, Janet Fisher and Tariq Latif. (Sample copy — £2.90). *Verse* is a Scottish based A5 poetry and criticism paperback of considerable strength. Edited by a team which includes Henry Hart, David Kinloch and the poet Robert Crawford, the magazine mixes local and international poets, features interviews and regional surveys, gives space to long poems and is not afraid of the avant garde. Typical poets include Geoff Hattersley, Penelope Shuttle, Jim Burns, Simon Armitage, Christopher Reid, Douglas Dunn and Tom Paulin. (Sample copy— £3.00.)

Chapter Nine

Specialist Poetry Mags
Clans, Denominations And Cabals

What do poetry magazines look like? Are most of them like *The Poetry Review*, a well-designed, intellectually respectable, double-column chunky? Or are there some which look more like *Old More's Almanac* or *Exchange And Mart*? How big should they be? The size of the *Daily Telegraph*, or like those Bibles which used to be advertised in the *Daily Mirror* classifieds — fully legible yet no bigger than a postage stamp? Over the years the commercial magazine trade has standardised on something which will fit neatly onto newsagents' shelves. The leisure industry is big business. Every human activity has its specialist periodical. The A4 standard is the paper size of the age. Non-commercial literary journals determined to be fashionable or simply keen on the economics of conformity have followed suit — *PN Review, The Rialto*. A number have opted for the *Poetry Review* double-column compromise which gives them shelf-life, while the rest remain traditionally pocket sized — *Agenda, Lallans, Poetry Ireland Review, Otter;* poster format — *Briggistane;* or, in the case of *Issue One*, small enough to file with your credit card.

Over the past decade advancing technology has improved production standards tenfold. Access to fast, graphics-efficient photocopiers has become common place, duplicators have vanished, everyone uses dot matrix printers or slick bubble jets, knowledge of word processing is rampant. Even the slightly-keen are now at home with data manipulation and desk top publishing. It is a production revolution of McLuhan-like significance. When the poems are submitted perfectly aligned and typed on carbon ribbon, they can hardly then be published looking worse. The gap between the print which you get in books and that which you are able to produce at home is closing fast. Luddites still stuck with their 30s manuals don't like it at all. One of the problems is that higher standards of production tend to make crap more credible. The power of print takes us over the top. Word processors on their own are bad enough because they make novelists garrulous, essayists verbose and poets never ending, but the latest classy replacement for Amstrad's bog-standard dot-matrix boneshaker, the ink jet printer, makes it all look so super real. Gone are the days when poetry mss lurched between publishers carved out in calligraphy, laboriously printed in HB pencil, illegibly tapped out on tiny italic typewriters, or once — in my own certain experience — set on a child's rubber stamp maker: not as much effort as you'd imagine though. They were haiku.

Gone too it seems, or fast going, are the highly irregular and often grossly amateur poetry productions on the little mag scene. No longer will we be anarchically assailed by the faded purple and sweet smelling spirit duplicated print of *Bogg* magazine. Nor will we anymore be presented with overlarge bunches of duplicated foolscap inadequately bound by tiny wire staples. Ken Geering's *Breakthru* magazine always came apart in your hands. Steve Pereira tried to solve the problem with an overlarge issue of *Angel Exhaust* by holding it together with nails. The editors of *Hanging Loose* didn't even bother. Some progressives shoved the lot into plastic bags and sold them as rather arty poetry packages — Bob Cobbing did this with *And*. Others went a stage further and bound up copies inside sheets of wallpaper, between bits of plywood packing cases, and on one memorable occasion between pieces of carpet sample. My copy came in royal blue Wilton, I recall. The most outstanding of all innovators was clearly Opal L. Nations with his aptly named magazine of the creative fringe, *Strange Faeces*. At one stroke he solved little mag storage problems for the foreseeable future by binding a wire coat-hanger into the spine. *Strange Faeces* were not to be kept on shelves. They were to be hung in the wardrobe with your shirts.

Poetry mags are by their nature hard to pigeon-hole but the broad categories outlined in Chapter Eight will suffice to give a general picture. Beneath the thin layer of UK national or semi-national poetry journals like *PN Review, Poetry Review, Agenda*, and *Ambit* lie a large number of magazines devoted either to the literature of a specific part of the UK — *Poetry Durham, New Welsh Review* — or work of a particular style, group or faction — *Ostinato* (the poetry of jazz), *Kroklok* (sound poetry), *Psychopoetica* (psychologically based verse). The range of competence in both writing and production is immense. What follows here are a few glances rather than a total survey, but they should give an idea of the general picture.

Scotland boasts a number of well tested, long-lived journals, and so it should. *Lines Review,* 'the oldest continuing Scottish literary magazine', was begun in 1952 and still owes a lot to the 50s for its design, if not its content. The current editor Tessa Ransford is keen on broadening the Scottish base as much as possible by including new voices together with work from further afield. "The poetry is nearly all unsolicited", she told me, "the reviews are careful and thorough, avoiding round-ups. I try not to have all the same names appear in all the magazines and I try to produce poetry that is serious, well-written and uses language skilfully, being accessible nonetheless to the intelligent, educated reader". Recent issues have included a 40th anniversary celebration number, an issue devoted to German poets in translation, along with work from the Gaelic, new poetry by Alan Jackson, Tom Buchan, Iain Crichton Smith, Angus Watson plus non-Scottish contributiors like Vuyelwa Carlin, Richard Hammersley and Chris Bendon. At 60 pages for £1.80, it's a bargain.

Lallans, 'the magazine for writing in Lowland Scots', makes terrific reading even if you can't fully understand most of the words. A recent editorial informed me that "Thir lest sax month haes seen a sicht mair interest in the Scots leid, an at the end o Februar, BBC Radio Scotland, follaein a walcum move bi Allan Jack, haed a 'Scots Language Week'...". The mag is an A5 mixture of similarly written poems, reviews and prose pieces. (Printit bi Dinwiddie Grieve Ltd, it costs £2 for a sample issue.)

Those wanting to complete their Scottish writing collection should also look at the exciting and often doorstop format *Edinburgh Review,* and Joy Hendry's excellent *Chapman* (sample copy — £2.70). This latter journal, billed as 'Scotland's Quality Literary Magazine', has moved on from its all-poetry 1970s origins to embrace the entire nation. "I like to think that what we have been doing has been lively and controversial, often taking the lead in the debate in what kind of contemporary Scottish culture we would like to see developing in the future — as well as publishing the best and most exciting of new writers," says the editor. Issues cover everything from international poetry to the Scots language. In addition the magazine runs a small press publishing first editions by new poets. A major northern enterprise.

Very loosely representing the North of England, Peter Sansom and Janet Fisher's *The North* is published by an organisation succinctly known as the 'poetry business'. Operating from offices in a restored Victorian arcade in Huddersfield, the Business acts as a resource centre and clearing house for information, runs day schools and workshops for poets, offers advice, selling down to earth analysis with its critical service and publishes books under the Smith/Doorstop imprint and, of course, the magazine. *The North* is more of a classic little in approach than many. It harbours few illusions about representing regional culture, sticking to newer, often unpublished poets set out in a lively looking double-column spread. Recent issues have mixed the likes of Geoff Hattersley, Nicki Jackowska and Neil Curry (who all have some sort of track record) with names totally new to me such as Sylvia Dann, Joe Fearn and Jenny Fidler. *The North* has solved the problems of dullness by being crisp and accessible and for the first time recently began to feature reviews. What it needs now is an underpinning of craft and a touch more style. (Sample copy — £2.75.)

Otter has a much smaller compass. Its new Devon poetry, packaged in a decently set A5 pamphlet, comes over as serious sub-Ted Hughes or self-consciously local — full of curlews, owls and foxes, hillsides and common ground. The style is traditional, with a fair regard for form. The editors are Richard Skinner (who also runs the neatly named self-enhancing *Dilettante Publications*), Edwyna Prior, Mark Beeson and Chris Southgate. (Sample copy — £1.80.)

Bedfordshire gets a good look in with the Eastern Arts supported *Spokes*. This is a quality production poetry and visual arts mag edited by Donald Atkinson and Sue Burrows which, although concentrating on local poets (Roy Blackman, Julius Smit, Daphne Craig, etc) seeks a 50/50 balance with work from elsewhere. A recent Bedford Readers' & Writers' Festival issue mixed it to perfection, putting Christopher Mills in with Selwyn Pritchard and Fiona Pitt-Kethley with Michael Bartholomew-Biggs. Amid the flashing of names it is hard to discern policy — be competent, make it look like a poem, send it in. (Sample copy — £4.00.)

Dave Woolley's arts magazine for the South West, *Westwords*, has similar production standards. Mainly poetry, some short fiction, and a reviews page, all leavened with moody black and white photography. The South West entry qualification gets overruled quite regularly. Recent issues have seen Graham Mort, Tom Kelly and arch small press poet Colin Nixon in there among the locals. (Sample copy — £2.50.)

Poetry Ireland Review, published by the Irish equivalent of the Poetry Society at The Austin Clarke Library, Dublin, is an upright, serious affair. Edited by a new man every four issues — Peter

Denman recently and now Pat Boran — it looks rather like *Poetry Wales* used to under J.P. Ward, but lacking that editor's style and interest in innovation. There are new poems from Irish stalwarts Peter Sirr, Eavan Boland, Patrick Gallagher and others; a certain openness to poets from outside Ireland such as Tony Curtis, Tessa Ransford and George Szirtes; Paula Meehan on what it's like to be a writer in residence; interviews with Carol Rumens, Ted Hughes and Joseph Brodsky, plus extensive reviews. Nothing too much to set the blood running, although I did take to Dennis O'Driscoll's 'Recent Poetry Pickings' — a selection of quotes on the art by the famous. Try these two:

> We all ought to be in prison now, because we tell the truth. I'm speaking as a Welshman...I ought to do the things that would land me in jail.
> — R.S. Thomas, speaking at a festival of East European Poetry, Radio 3.

> It seems to me that there are a million poets that write interesting verse, but I can't think of a single one that I would think of getting up in the morning to find my life profoundly changed and enlightened and deepened by.
> —A.R. Ammons in *Michigan Quarterly Review.*

Poetry Ireland Review costs £4.00 an issue. Its publishers also run an Irish poetry book club, publish a newsletter and allow public access to their extensive poetry library.

Moving about as far west as we can is *The Salmon*, styling itself as 'an international literary journal from the West of Ireland' and looking pretty presentable in its spine-bound typeset pocket format. The problem is that the work is neither deeply literary nor international enough to compete for long in the mainstream. Despite this there are good poems, mainly from Irish writers such as Liam Murphy and Ciaran O'Driscoll. There are quite a number of poems in Irish as well, some of them looking somewhat modern if layout is anything to go by. *The Salmon* also publish a guide to poetry publishing in Ireland listing some 27 newspapers and magazines as well as detailing their requirements. Price £2.50. The magazine costs £2.00.

Magazines which specialise in a particular genre, or promote the work of a faction or cabal, tend to be less well presented than journals serving geographic areas. *Psychopoetica* is a semi-annual stapled A4 collection of 'psychologically-based poetry' put out by Geoff Lowe from the Department of Psychology at the University of Hull. The total effect is as unusual as it is uneven. Amid what appear to be the full-blown ramblings of inmates lie poems inspired by everything from Alzheimer's disease to minimalism. The work comes from all over and is reproduced exactly in the form submitted, which makes a lot of it pretty illegible. The editor makes known a preference for short, experimental, unrhymed poetry, although much of what I read turned out to be not in the least innovative and reminded me strongly of the kind of work found in your average little little. *Psychopoetica* has its own spin-off publications, which so far have included an anthology of Yorkshire poets and a collection by Virginia V. James Hlavsa. (Sample copy — £1.50.)

First Offence, although it might look like it, is by no means an average little. The cover of issue 4, devoted to jazz related works, is an A4 dark mimeo smudge. This is not the Cobbing original I took it for, but a design by Ulli Freer. Issue 8, a general number featuring Allen Fisher, Paul Green, Maggie O'Sullivan and Gavin Selerie, among others, uses a design which looks like ploughed fields photographed from above. This time it is by Cobbing. *First Offence* deals not in poems but 'texts' and specialises in the work of progressive and experimental poets, as few magazines do in the UK at present. Editor Tim Fletcher knows his stuff, mixing American Language poets such as Clarke Coolidge with inhabitors of the UK cutting edge Ken Edwards, Tom Raworth, Wendy Mulford and Virginia Firnberg. Tough going if you are not a convert, but for the open minded worth it in the end. *Fragmente*, run by Andrew Lawson and Anthony Mellors, covers similar territory. 'A magazine of contemporary poetics', which means the whole post-modern marsh of verse, text, talk and critique. Geraldine Monk, Bill Griffiths, Peter Riley, Richard Caddel and Harry Gilonis are typical contributors. A5 production, with the financial aid of Southern Arts, is excellent.

Two further poetry periodicals, which are neither little in aspiration nor yet significant enough to be considered national, need to be mentioned. *Poetry Now* and *Envoi* are the two UK poetry magazines most often first encountered by the beginner and unfortunately are the ones by which many set their standards. *Poetry Now,* run by Ian and Tracey Walton at the Arrival Press is responsible for the vast series of regional poetry and short fiction anthologies which have been covering the UK for the past few years. Despite suspicions to the contrary, this is not a vanity operation. The Waltons are mining a seam. This is the literary equivalent of *The Sun. Poetry Now* is open to everything; an unthreatening multi-column mix of features, letters, news, notes, profile, quotation, and endless amoeba-like poetry. Jolly, smiling, and full of zest the magazine might be, but its standards still remain incredibly low. (Sample copy — £3.50.) The long-lived *Envoi* had a bad reputation under earlier editors for selecting work by committee and going for the lowest common denominator, but with Roger Elkin in charge things are changing fast. *Envoi* is a chunky looking paperback of reviews, competition information and news, plus a lot of poetry. Mostly it is new voices from the little arenas, but not exclusively. Issues I've seen have included Myra Schneider and Merryn Williams as well as Colin Nixon and Eddie Flintoff. (Sample copy — £2.00.)

Rustic Rub is Jay Woodman's all-poetry successor to her excellent environmental mag *And What Of Tomorrow?* The new one uses groups of verse by several poets, drawn mostly from the little mag arenas so far although but new voices are an increasing priority.

British mags in the field of specialisation are much scarcer than one might think. With the exception of journals devoted to the works of specific writers, such as *The Kipling Journal, The Powys Review,* and the *Byron Journal,* we fall well behind the Americans, who have poetry magazines for everything from haiku to concrete and Christianity to epigrams. For further information on specialist literary magazines check the British Council's discursive *British Literary Periodicals — A Selected Bibliography* introduced by Anthony Thwaite (British Council, 10 Spring Gardens, London, SW1A 2BN). Addresses for the magazines discussed here are to be found in Appendix V.

Chapter Ten

The Little Littles —
The Small Magazines

How old do you have to be to get published? Does it matter? Robert Peters in his *Black and Blue Guides To Current Literary Journals* (Dustbooks) has identified a trend. "The darling poets of these journals are almost exclusively under 50 years of age — the ripe decade runs from, say, 35 to 45", which says something not so much about the age of poets actually writing, but the age of those bothering to send their stuff around. In Wales you are young if you are under 39. This was one of the entrance qualifications for the anthology I edited with Meic Stephens, *Green Horse (Christopher Davies)*. Go beyond this turning point and your *Selected Poems* appear, you are asked to chair committees, whole issues of magazines are devoted to your work. What actually happens when you pass 40 (or 45 in the States — these things are forever fluid) is that you give up bothering with stamped addressed envelopes and only send to friendly places, where you've been asked, where you know the editor, where they like your work. Any why not? The indignity of rejection is harder to bear among the increasing prides of age. The editor of *Poetry Wales* sends back a perfectly good poem for no apparent reason. You wish to set fire to his coat.

Peters, who is pretty good at tearing the pomposity of the literary scene apart, has identified what he regards as the most common types of poem published by respectable journals: "the Ego Poem; trivialities from a poet's life; the old folks at home poem — excursions into sentimental memories of family and friends; a poet's cute rite of passage to manhood or womanhood; the coy bucolic vapid imitators of...(Peters cites William Stafford and Robert Frost for whom we'll substitute Dylan and R.S. Thomas); the dying relatives poem; the reportage style, in which poems generate themselves around tedious journal entries — the day book poem is one of the disasters to appear in the past decade or so; and finally the academic abroad poem". To these I could well add the tramp poem, the down-trodden socialist poem, the coming to terms with the language poem, as well as the historical biography as piece of verse. No doubt you'll have your own favourites. The advice seems to be that if you need to get on, be published and win competitions then do not be ultimately original. Be round about 40. Follow an existing trend. Otherwise it's the wild, woolly world of the little little; the backbone of all poetry publishing; the one-person, biased, stubbornly persistent and generally incorrigible small magazine.

On the British scene such journals proliferate. There does not seem to be a town or a writing group without its own. Andy Warhol's prediction has come true. Anyone, anywhere, talented or not, can become famous, albeit within their own circle, for at least 15 minutes. For many this is all they want.

To be fair many littles turn out to be significantly more than mere outlets for their egotistical contributors. If you pick your way with care you will come across taste, knowledge, style and certainly experimentation. In the absence of anything other than the pervasive greyness promoted by an all powerful poetry mafia, which for many is all mainstream poetry publishing is, then the cutting edge of verse in the UK has to be with the littles.

It would be nice to be able to suggest a shop somewhere where many of these raggedy swatches of innovative wisdom could be seen in one go but the Thatcher years have seen off Bob Cobbing at Better Books and Nick Kimberley at Compendium. Bernard Stone is, of course, an institution, Alan Halsey keeps his hand in at the Poetry Bookshop, Hay-on-Wye, as I do for now at Oriel, but the best route is directly. Send for a few copies by post.

Chapter Nine covered the mainstream national poetry mags; Chapter Ten looks at specialist and regional journals. The clutch of mags surveyed here have been selected somewhat arbitrarily from the hundreds of others available. This is the great advantage with small mags — if you don't like it, there is always another. If it turns you down, send your work off to the next one on the list.

TOPS, run off by bubble-jet printer, appears in three A5 sections: *Toadbird, Canto* and the unfortunately named *Cowpat*: "If you feel compelled to tell me that my little magazine is a piece of shit, you are too late; I got there first". The mags are published by editor Alex Anderson's 'Campaign to Restore Authentic Poetry (C.R.A.P.)' and have been appearing for years. This is the heart of classic little magdom, where the central issue is never the quality, nor the direction, but simply getting the work out. What is important is not what you say but the cost of the stamps you've stuck onto your SAE. Rejection slips are treasured rarities. But I am being too hard. Peter Russell publishes here, so do Eddie Flintoff, Gerald England, Michael O'Higgins, Jane Fell, Dewi Hopkins, Odubo Pereowei and dozens more — all enjoying themselves enormously. *TOPS* stands for The Old Police Station, the magazine's base at 80 Lark Lane, Liverpool, L17 8UU.

Purple Patch, run for 50 issues over the last 15 years by Geoff Stevens from West Bromwich, would have been dismissed as a *TOPS* clone, were it not for the editor's eccentric visuals and the addition of a gossip column. The problem with this otherwise brilliant idea is the quality of the bits of rumour and outrage Stevens prints — although I did like the report on the editor who screws up rejected poems before putting them back into their envelopes. Apart from this it's Michael Newman, Steve Sneyd, and Betty Paskin all over again. The literary equivalent of satellite tv.

Iota, run by David Holliday, is an admirable successor to his very similar magazine of the 60s and 70s, *Script*. Set by word processor and printed by offset the magazine has a quiet authority and carries around 50 poems per issue, of which 20 or so are by newcomers. Holliday's guiding principles are to publish no work by the editor and to only allow others one poem per issue: "Spreads encouragement, avoids the danger of getting into a rut". The fare is as one might expect: Colin Nixon, George Parfitt, Alun Rees, Brian Vincent et al, and, there in the middle, totally unexpectedly, the great Arthur Winfield Knight recalling his beat days with Miller in Montmartre and Hemingway on the Left Bank. (Sample copy — £1.00.)

Bogg, edited by George Cairncross from North Yorkshire, has been around for decades. When it began it was produced to varying degrees of illegibility on a spirit duplicator. The high-spot of many a young poet's career was to have their work appear, gloriously unreadable, in Cairncross's school-exam-paper smelling magazine. You could publish the same poem elsewhere simultaneously without worry, no one would be able to tell. But how things have changed. *Bogg*, well into seventy issues, is today a tidily lithoed "Anglo-American journal" with an American address and co-owner along with editorial outposts in Australia, New Zealand and Canada. All this means that the traditional amateur little mag flavour has become supplanted by more international concerns. Jon Silkin contributes, as does Jim Burns. On the other hand there is still loads of chat, extracts from readers' letters, reviews, drawings, articles, round-ups, essays, making it a bright if never quite authoritative assemblage. Under the lively veneer still lurks the *Bogg* of old. Colin Nixon, Andy Darlington, Derrick Butress, Pete Faulkner — where have we read these guys before?

Eric Ratcliffe has been publishing *Ore* since 1955. For a small mag longevity on this scale is hard to achieve. Ratcliffe is not interested in poetry for its own sake which might account for the considerable number of non-poets among his readers. *Ore* centres on ancient Britain, its content has a "synthetic atmosphere of legend, a belief in 'soul', a leaning towards heritage". It favours earth-sciences, druids, standing stones, Arthurian legends, dowsers, ley hunters, voyagers, spiritual explorers. One would expect it to be a collection of articles, essays and historical exploration. Not so. *Ore* is primarily a poetry magazine. The issue I have to hand has a poem to the greater stitchwort by Brian Mitchell, Daphne Philips on Cadbury, spiritual polymorphs from Pamela Constantine plus numerous other craggy, dark-age adventurers. Nice to see a consistently different approach, and, like British Telecom, his continuing success has even enabled the editor to bring the subscription price down. (Sample copy — £1.45.) Small press coverage is immense.

Borderlines, magazine of the rather grand sounding 'Anglo-Welsh Poetry Society', which the editors admit really ought to be the 'England-Wales Border Area Poetry Society', turns out to be a rather local magazine of creative writing from the border around Shrewsbury. Editorship is now in the hands of Dave Bingham and Kevin Bamford, helped by a voluntary panel of members who have enlarged the format to B5 and expanded their horizons to include good work sent in from anywhere. Recent typewriter-set issues have included Mike Jenkins, Vuyelwa Carlin, Rose Flint, David Barnett, Chris Bendon and others, plus a couple of Biblical pieces by Kevin Bamford translated *into* Welsh by Huw Richards. (Sample copy — £1.00.)

Krax, run by Andy Robson for the past twenty-one years from 63 Dixon Lane, Leeds, LS12 4RR, is home of the non-academic, light-hearted poem titled things like 'Sausages Rule O.K.', 'Duel with a public telephone box' and 'The Poet Looks At Forty From Behind A Big Cushion'. These get written in relaxed moments by the standard little mag roster of Andy Darlington, David Caddy, Colin Nixon, Josephine Austin, Glenda Winlein and company. You don't laugh too much after you've read them, rather you twitch a bit. At least I did. Half the print run goes to the States and in quiet moments Robson extends his touch to booklets, some tiny (Tina Fulkner's *Impermanent Glamour* will fit a shirt cuff), others serious (Lyn Lifshin & Belinda Subraman's *Skin Divers* hits the intimate rather than the humorous). *Krax* runs to a bus timetable, always several months late. Be warned.

The Wide Skirt is one of the better littles. Good title, good production and a consistently high standard of innovative writing, usually with something to say or a new way of saying it. Editor Geoff Hattersley is a kind of Carcanetless Ian McMillan whose approach to poetry is, if not literary, at least pretty catholic. The work included has a northern feel to it, a gritty directness lacking from much other small mag material. Jim Burns contributes one of the funniest of his I've ever read, while Alan Dent moralises from the edges. Elsewhere it's Yann Lovelock, Liz Loxley, Sue Dymoke, Ian McMillan, Michael Blackburn et al — all readable, and in a few cases memorable too.

Staple, a solid, well produced pocketful of new poetry edited by Donald Measham and Bob Windsor, began as a bunch of stapled sheets and is now the polished pride of the East Midlands. Content tends towards the fresh, accessible and crafted, with a determined lean away from the superstar circuit. Recognisable names are rare, tone is serious, the poetry is not chuck-away verse. *Staple* runs its own open poetry competition, produces a successful series of poetry postcards as well as books in the *Staple First Editions* series. Potential contributors to this part of the operation pay a small reading fee, in exchange for which they get a 250 word critical report.

David Crystal's *Dog* runs "poetry and short fiction, life lived in cities, dazzling narratives on the urban experience and no haiku. Essentially the art of subversion". The mag has trouble with postmen who think it's a canine operation. "I gave the woman a good kicking..." begins one poem, "He wakes at six o'clock, head aching, tongue furred" starts another. Bobby Christie, Geoff Hattersley and Martin Myers get their work included here.

Ramraid Extra Ordinaire sounds like the child of the 90s it is. Editor Kerry Sowerby aims for writing which "at least attempts at something new", and the edgy readability of the mag seems to bear his success out. "I can hear the neighbours' TV through the connecting wall / so in return I play them a selection of modern music" writes Martin Stannard. It sums up Sowerby's approach.

THE LITTLE LITTLES

Tony Frazer's excellent *Shearsman* comes in by mail from Chile, routed via his UK base at 47 Dayton Close, Plymouth, PL6 5DX. Frazer avoids the whole business of bulk and tardiness by sticking to 16 unbound A5 pages at a time. His taste is eclectic, with a strong interest in the Harry Guest, Peter Riley, Yann Lovelock and Larry Eigner version of post-modernism backed with numerous translations, often from the French. This is a magazine to read rather than contribute to. Pushes boundaries, opens the mind. (Sample copy — £1.00) *Shearsman Books* put out slightly more substantial publications by the likes of Nathaniel Tarn, Roy Fisher and George Evans. *Shearsman* stablemate *Oasis*, run by Ian Robinson, is a very similar magazine, a dozen typed pages of undeniable quality, but not a patch on the engaging journal it was decades ago. Robinson casts a wide international net, making me think contributors would have a better chance if they lived in Norway than Wales.

There are plenty of other littles worth spending time with; almost as many as there are worth throwing away. *Foolscap*, which is actually A5 size, a classic old style small mag run by Judi Benson; *Quartos* which mixes guidance to writers with snatches of poetry (and some of the poets should heed the guidance); *Pennine Platform*, Brian Merrikin Hill's long-lived and by no means exclusively Yorkshire 32 pager; *The Frogmore Papers*, the tiny outgrowth of the Folkestone Tea Rooms' poetry group; *Odyssey*, Derrick Woolf's splendid mag and press operating out of Coleridge Cottage; *Acumen*, Patricia Oxley's serious assault on the poetry scene: a major little if there ever was one. Most little mags end with a review section, giving poetry news and listing other similar operations. To keep ahead look here. And don't give up.

Some poets revel in the littles, others wouldn't be seen dead. For a number they represent the only available outlet. That they exist and flourish is a healthy sign. Literary repression hasn't got to us yet.

Chapter Eleven

The Book In Hand —
Commercial And Specialist Publishers

For the poet, a book in hand is always regarded as better than a whole series of appearances in magazines. It's a goal; for many *the* goal — the collection, the tome, a slim volume devoted entirely to yourself. How those who have not yet succeeded desire one. The book becomes an obsession.

In terms of readership, magazines undoubtedly reach more people. A good poem in *Poetry Wales* will do your reputation more good than the same work embedded deeply in a poorly circulated first volume. Publish regularly in *Poetry Review* and you will reach thousands. A book, even a good seller, will be unlikely to reach half as many.

Such statistics cut little ice. The book with your name on the cover becomes the only thing worth having. The rush to find a publisher is suddenly the most vital thing in the world. New poets with stars in their eyes never realize what a difficult, heartless, ego-crushing road they have embarked on. "Your work has been read by our editors and is unfortunately not suitable for our needs." Why the hell not? Finding a publisher in the 90s is as hard as finding a plumber on a Sunday.

Where do you begin? Your personal library of slim volumes all appear to have been produced by publishers who no longer exist or who have long since given up an interest in verse. Who are Cape Golliard? Why have Routledge and Kegan Paul sent Peter Redgrove packing? Down what river have Rapp and Whiting sailed? Who has swallowed Latimer New Dimensions? And what of the publisher of Glyn Jones, Bryn Griffiths, Welsh Voices, *The Lilting House* and that evergreen gnarled bard Dylan Thomas? J.M. Dent — London bolt-hole for the blossoming Anglo-Welsh — reduced now to a mere imprint of the Orion group, used only for Dylan softback re-runs and expensive 'collecteds' of R.S.

Penguin, who knock out paperbacks with a commercial edge, may seem a likely target. Not only do they publish highly successful anthologies of contemporary verse including Blake Morrison and Andrew Motion's *Penguin Book of Contemporary Poetry* and Edward Lucie Smith's *British Poetry Since 1945,* but produce individual volumes by present day British poets as diverse as Dannie Abse, Roger McGough and Jeremy Reed. Forget it. They have no desire to see *Eighteen Poetic Thoughts* by Glyn Parry Jones of Ystradgynlais.

Present policy is to actively dissuade poets from sending in unsolicited collections. Books are scooped up from the lists of specialists and reissued in snazzy paperback form. To get on board you must be like D.M. Thomas, Tony Harrison and Peter Redgrove and first establish your reputation elsewhere.

As few as six UK publishers in the commercial field actively publish more than the occasional volume of poetry today and to the outsider most of that appears to be backlist. It helps fire the grand conspiracy theory. There are two great wheels in poetry. Those on the inner one are all publishers, editors, run magazines or are important reviewers. Their wheel spins in golden light. The other, the big one with the rest of us clinging to its edges, that one spins in Dante-like darkness.

Commercial Publishers

Faber and Faber is the publisher most associated with poetry, although its money these days comes from cookbooks, travel guides and volumes on wine. T.S. Eliot's great period as editor has given Faber a backlist of unassailable quality. Contemporaries include Ted Hughes, Seamus Heaney, Andrew Motion, Douglas Dunn. Under the present poetry editor, Christopher Reid, policy is to expand the number of volumes by new poets — Martin Turner, Harry Smart and Lavinia Greenlaw have arrived this way — but in total their numbers remain small. The Chatto and Windus list was revived by Andrew Motion and is now in the hands of poetry whizz-kid Simon Armitage. Alan Jenkins, Selima Hill, Carol Rumens, Norman McCaig and Robert Crawford are staples. Hutchinson, under Tony Wittome's editorship, have become considerably slowed by the recession, but expect a revival soon. They like to see work from new poets, but rarely get the chance to use it. Mainstays are Dannie Abse, Gavin Ewart and Kit Wright. Oxford University Press holds a central position in the publishing of British poetry with its enviable range of historic, classic and thematic anthologies. Editor Jacqueline Simms works hard to keep up the contemporary end with an extensive series of 'Oxford Poets' which includes Jo Shapcott, Stephen Romer, Brad Leithauser, Carole Satyamurti and Chris Wallace-Crabb. With editor Robin Robertson's move across from Secker & Warburg to Jonathan Cape, the latter's 60s glory appears to be restored. Most of the Secker poets have followed and there have been new captures too. Adam Thorpe, Tom Leonard, Peter Redgrove, Vicki Feaver and Sharon Olds all hang their hats here. Christopher Sinclair-Stevenson's Sinclair-Stevenson imprint is a recent commercial arrival, which puts out around eight poetry titles per year. The mix is ancient and modern, with a penchant for humorous verse. Poets include Jon Silkin, Ruth Fainlight, Selwyn Pritchard and Anne McManus.

Other Possibilities

Among the paperback houses the HarperCollins imprint, Paladin, looked good for a while with its Iain Sinclair-edited series of volumes by poetry's outsiders, but the recession has seen an end to all that. Chris Torrance and Barry MacSweeney pulped. Terrible news. Reed International's Minerva has brought out a Les Murray collected and may do others. Edinburgh University Press produce volumes of Scottish interest under the Polygon imprint. Both Virago and The Women's Press have a policy to publish the occasional women's interest volume with Virago running a series of anthologies of new women poets. Sometimes poetry appears on the lists of Michael Joseph, Robert Hale, Robson Books, Harvill and Dent, but it's tokenism. Determined poets will need to look elsewhere.

The Specialists

Hard commercial decisions have never been the friends of verse. "And give up verse, my boy, There's nothing in it" pronounced Ezra Pound, which as we've seen is what most of the big boys do. The way out of the thicket is to achieve subsidy. Of the number who have managed this, seven stand out as more successful than their contemporaries and can now be said by now to dominate the 'respectable' market. Their books are as good looking as anything produced by the commercial trade. Carcanet, Bloodaxe, Seren, Anvil, and Peterloo are all well supported by either Arts Council or Arts Board. Enitharmon and Littlewood Arc get some help but for various reasons less than the others. They move forward by sticking to what they know best.

Carcanet Press

Leader of the pack, intellectual elder and perhaps the most commercially run, is Carcanet. It was established in 1969 as an outgrowth of Michael Schmidt's undergraduate magazine of the same name (Carcanet lit. — a linked, jewelled necklace). The press ran from a backroom at Pin Farm, Oxford. Schmidt, along with partner Peter Jones, was lit by that which fires many small press operators, a feeling "that good poetry was being wilfully ignored by the major publishers". He wanted to put the publishing world to rights. His early successes were with Octavio Paz, Charles Tomlinson and Donald Davie. Being president of the Oxford University Poetry Society helped with the contacts, as did his new and much grander magazine *Poetry Nation* (later to develop into the influential *PN Review*).

The Press moved to Manchester in 1975 and turned fast from short range pamphleteering to full frontal book publication. Elizabeth Jennings, Christopher Middleton, Michael Hamburger, Edwin Morgan and C.H. Sisson joined the fold. By the 80s the press had expanded to cover essays, anthologies, novels and translations. It was a success; so much so that Schmidt began to find capital restraints a problem, the classic dilemma of the small business. Important titles were being offered, which he simply could not afford to publish. Help came in the shape of Robert Gavron, who effectively bought out the imprint but retained Schmidt as editor. New staff were appointed, an office was opened in New York and fiction publishing was expanded vigorously. Important new poets, notably Gillian Clarke, John Ash and Frank Kuppner, continued to join the list.

Today Carcanet can hardly be considered a traditional small press. It has over 500 titles in print, uses commercial warehousing and has reps in 42 countries. It publishes titles from all quarters. New poets are welcome to send in so long as they enclose an SAE. Carcanet persists in keeping its writers' work in print. It concentrates on substantial editions — which make whole oeuvres available — and cheap selected poems, which serve both as an introduction to a writer's work and a way of keeping their best poems before a wider public.

Overall one gets a feeling of studied seriousness from Schmidt's brainchild. Carcanet is not leader of fashion, no popularizer, yet its service to poetry is immeasurable.

Arc Publications

Regional bias can be a positive asset in the formation of a list. The Arc Publications imprint, based at the Nanholme Centre in Lancashire, has a strong interest in northern writing in all its manifestations. The imprint results from the merger of John and Carole Killick's Littlewood Press with printer Tony Ward's much older (although considerably less active) Arc Publications. Arc's best selling Ivor Cutler titles now enhance a sturdy catalogue which includes Wes Magee, Philip Callow, Theresa Tomlinson and Graham Mort. Killick's recent departure and problems with funding have been weathered with the appointment of poets Michael Hulse and David Morley as associate editors. The list is now a fine amalgam of Northern grit with contemporary zing. Where else would you find Maura Dooley, Anna Adams, Bob Cobbing and Jeff Nuttall all happily emerging from the same door? The excellent production comes from having a printer in charge. Policy is to produce at least ten titles annually. Beginners welcome, but Ward insists they should look at his company's product first.

Enitharmon Press

For quiet class and understated style we should turn to the mother of Orc, Blake's Enitharmon. Begun in 1969 by bookdealer Alan Clodd, the Enitharmon Press has moved forward almost by stealth. The editions are produced to the highest of standards, the best by any British poetry press. Their selection of poets is solid, well away from fashion and always worth reading. "Poetry of the human spirit", "moral imagination" and "intellectual focus" are the kind of phrases used in the press's brochures, and they go some way to describe a publisher who has rescued David Gascoyne from obscurity, salvaged John Heath-Stubb's *Artorius* from rejection by *OUP*, and rediscovered Kathleen Raine's *The Faces of Day and Night*. Under

Clodd's immaculate directorship Enitharmon brought out Vernon Watkins, Edmund Blunden, Frances Horovitz, and John Moat, among others, along with Ceri Richards' remarkable illustrated version of Dylan Thomas's *Collected Poems*. On Clodd's retirement the Press was passed on to one of his editors, Stephen Stuart-Smith, who has managed to simultaneously maintain quality while doubling output, all with the same Clodd-like attention to detail. Under the new regime Enitharmon has remained a fad-free oasis of quality. It promotes new writers, revives the reputations of neglected ones and acts as an outlet for those disenchanted by the commercial opposition. The current list includes Jeremy Hooker, Jeremy Reed, Edwin Brock, Ruth Pitter and Martyn Crucefix, a series of volumes which mix poets and artists, plus a new set of pamphlets. Stuart-Smith stresses his openness to the work of new writers, citing the cases of Crucefix, Hilary Davies and Kim Taplin, all of whom have received praise from the critics. His circulation figures, which he regards as "ridiculously modest", are actually just as good as those of his competitors. An excellent taster comes in the form of the *An Enitharmon Anthology* (1990), a tribute to Alan Clodd, which includes a fine cross section of "moral imagination" from Enitharmon writers and their supporters.

Peterloo Poets

The alternative to the mainstream does not have to be the adventurous avant garde. Harry Chambers has made his reputation proving this to be the case. His Peterloo Poets has, since the mid-seventies, devoted itself to finding new writers whose work is "accessible to all who can read and have feelings". Described by Peter Forbes as "the purest of poetry lists," Harry Chambers' press makes a virtue out of publishing the unknown. Begun as an extension of the 60s magazine *Phoenix*, the early pamphlets by the then unknown poets Peter Scupham, John Mole, Seamus Heaney and Derek Mahon, soon turned into substantial, well designed volumes. Chambers' declared preference for "poetry that is rhythmically alive but syntactically correct...written in language that is in touch with the language of the age" has won him support across a broad front. A recent book *The Hen Ark* by Mark Roper is not only a joint publication with Eire's

Salmon Publishing but has financial assistance from The Arts Council Incentive Fund, South West Arts and Cornwall County Council, plus a Ralph Lewis Award from the University of Sussex. The press's audited accounts must have wide circulation. Policy is to publish at least six new volumes per year, together with the irregular *Peterloo Preview* which provides an introduction to the work of half a dozen new additions to the stable. The current volume carries Robert Hull, Michael Laskey, Neal Mason, Mark Roper, Rosamund Stanhope and Pamela Stewart. Chambers casts his net wide, and is aided in his endeavours by the annual Peterloo Poetry Competition (sponsored by Marks and Spencer), as well as numerous other joint ventures with bodies such as the Arvon Foundation and Minority Arts Advisory Service. If having "no enthusiasm for too much cleverness or obscurity" proves anything, it is that accessibility sells books. Peterloo's successes are on a grand scale — more than 3000 copies of U.A. Fanthorpe's *Side Effects* (a poet later signed by Penguin), the same for *An Enormous Yes*, a selection of tributes to Larkin, and 2000 plus for *Boo To A Goose* and *Mad Parrot*, two volumes of John Mole's poetry for children. All this from a husband and wife team operating out of a cottage in Cornwall.

Peterloo's poets, if not outsiders in the maverick sense of that word, are certainly not on the inner wheel. Recent books have been from Dana Gioia, Michael Laskey and Mike Harding. Who are the press's mainstays? Late starters, competition winners, writers from the regions. Try them. You could well be surprised.

Anvil Press Poetry

Peter Jay's Anvil Press is another product of the 60s. In the early days it was a classic alternative publisher, a founder member of the ALP, and home for many of the exciting new works then being produced by the children of albion. Harry Guest began here, as did Gavin Bantock, Philip Holmes, Anthony Howell, Heather Buck and Richard Burns. Peter Levi, Oxford Professor of Poetry, was an early catch. Over the years, Jay's insistence on quality and style together with an abiding interest in translated poetry has shifted the Press away from formal opposition and into an unfashionable but distinctive arena all of its own. Some might accuse him of losing his way among the grants and the Europeans but he still publishes Harry

Guest, brought out John Welch's remarkable *Out Walking* and is a fervent supporter of surrealist John Digby. Pamphlet series have been replaced by sturdy anthologies — *Anvil New Poets* presents the work of nine newcomers. Jay and his assistant try to bring out at least a dozen titles per year: "Doing our best according to eclectic lights," he calls it. "We respond to what we can, at present a lot of that seems to be coming from abroad". His greatest successes have been Alistair Eliot's translation of Verlaine's erotic *Femmes/Hombres,* George Seferis's *Complete Poems*, Michael Hamburger's *Unofficial Rilke* and the complete *Baudelaire*, topped by a totally home grown talent, Carol Ann Duffy. Her *Standing Female Nude* is now into its third printing. Her *Selling Manhattan* and *The Other Country* and the prize winning *Mean Time*, are all heading that way. "Spirit of the age", says Jay.

Bloodaxe Books

Bloodaxe Books, run from Newcastle upon Tyne, like to think of themselves as revolutionaries. Begun little over a decade ago with a pamphlet by Ken Smith, the press now reckon to sell more poetry than anyone except OUP, Penguin and Faber. Like many small publishers, founder Neil Astley had become disillusioned with a scene run, as he saw it, by academics, full of dust and boredom. Where were the voices which would lift the hairs on the back of his neck? The innovative Europeans, the ignored Northerners, the whole post-*Briggflatts* push of contemporary writing? Bloodaxe, named after the last great Viking King, set out to find them. After a decade oscillating between overwhelming success and disastrous failure (in 1985 their distributor, Noonan Hurst, collapsed owing Bloodaxe a small fortune) the evidence is that they have managed it. Winner of the *Sunday Times* Small Publisher of the Year Award 1990, the company now lead where many would otherwise be afraid to follow. Astley and his partner, Simon Thirsk, mix world figures with upstart newcomers. Irina Ratushinskaya's *No, I'm Not Afraid* has sold an amazing 20,000 copies; Jeni Couzyn's *Contemporary Women Poets* anthology runs close behind. They published Tony Harrison's *V* long before Channel 4 even considered running it and signed R.S. Thomas from under the noses of the native Welsh. Their record with first timers is enviable: Simon Armitage, Glyn Maxwell, Helen Dunmore, and Nigel Wells all began here. Their output is prodigious: 70 new titles announced in their current catalogue, more than 250 books in print.

For the present their financial support is secure, but as a hedge against future difficulties Astley intends to broaden his approach: "We do need to diversify our list into some areas which will help support the poetry". Like a number of the other specialists, Bloodaxe is now looking at fiction, literary criticism, cultural studies and local books. The poetry, though, *will* remain central. "Our aim is to reflect the full range of contemporary poetry in our publishing, and to keep taking on new writers, older new poets as well as young new poets. Bloodaxe thrives on new blood."

Current bestsellers include Benjamin Zephaniah, Paul Hyland, Jackie Kay, Attila The Stockbroker, Ian Duhig, Medbh McGuckian, C.K. Williams, Lemn Sissay, Adrian Mitchell, Sappho and Brendan Kennelly, plus their controversial anthology *The New Poetry*. For a good taster of *Bloodaxe* poetry, try their *Poetry With An Edge*.

Seren

Closer to home, Seren is the name to look for. Begun as Poetry Wales Press in 1981 by the then editor of that magazine, Cary Archard, its first two titles were new collections by Mike Jenkins and Nigel Jenkins. Archard was keen to extend the work of the magazine and to fill the gaping hole in Anglo-Welsh publishing with exciting new images of Wales. His vision was a press which would consolidate the local culture, revitalize neglected poets, hunt out new voices and set Wales' creative output up as a viable alternative to that emanating from London. Central to the achievement of these ends has been the Welsh Arts Council block grant which has enabled him to appoint staff, (notably Managing Director Mick Felton and poetry editor Amy Wack), run an office, to commission work and to compete on common ground with the likes of Gillian Clarke's publisher, Carcanet. At first the press ran from rooms at Dannie Abse's cottage at Ogmore, but increasing turnover soon saw the need to move to more formal offices on one of Bridgend's industrial estates and subsequently into the town itself.

As a success story, Seren's matches that of Bloodaxe. Its editions are well produced, immaculately designed and actively promoted. The press use professional representation and distribution, have agents in eight countries and sell significant quantities in North

America. The current catalogue runs to more than 150 titles, some 70 or so of which are poetry. Seren mix the established with the upcoming, producing an attractive series of selected poems which aim to keep in print the core of Anglo-Welsh writing and back all this up with a solid range of anthologies. New voices are regarded as vital to their operation. Their best-seller is the classic Garlick/Mathias *Anglo-Welsh Poetry 1480-1990* with over 3000 copies in print, followed closely (and surprisingly) by Jean Earle's *Visiting Light*. Most, but not all, poets of significance writing in Wales have by now achieved a Seren publication: John Ormond, John Tripp, Tony Curtis, Glyn Jones, Christopher Meredith, Robert Minhinnick, Sheenagh Pugh — the list is long. Typical poets include Paul Henry, Peter Finch, John Powell Ward, Steve Griffiths, John Davies, Menna Elfyn and Ruth Bidgood.

The way forward for Seren, as for Carcanet and Bloodaxe, is to enlarge the base. More novels, essays, playscripts, criticism, biography, titles from outside Wales too (Vuyelwa Carlin, Rose Flint, Desmond Graham) — more income generating material to help support the poetry. "Poetry just doesn't sell enough," Mick Felton told me. It is a familiar story.

Where To Find Out More

Never submit blindly. Research the market. Buy some books, read through the range of what is available and see where you might fit in. Send for the publisher's catalogues. In Wales you will find a good, browsable selection at Oriel. The full range of publishers' addresses can be found in both Macmillan's *Writer's Handbook* and A & C Black's *Writer's & Artist's Yearbook*. Those mentioned in the text you have just read are as follows:

Commercial And Specialist Publishers Of Poetry

Anvil Press Poetry, 69 King George Street, London, SE10 8PX.
Bloodaxe Books Ltd, PO Box 1SN, Newcastle upon Tyne, NE99 1SN.
Jonathan Cape, (a division of Random House Publishing Group Ltd),
    Random House, 20 Vauxhall Bridge Road, London, SW1V 2SA.
Carcanet Press Ltd, 208 Corn Exchange Buildings, Manchester, M4
    3BG.

Chatto & Windus, (a division of Random House Publishing Group Ltd), Random House, 20 Vauxhall Bridge Road, London, SW1V 2SA.

Enitharmon Press, 36 St George's Avenue, London, N7 0HD.

Faber and Faber, 3 Queens Square, London, WC1N 3AU.

Robert Hale, Clerkenwell House, 45-47 Clerkenwell Green, London, EC1R 0HT.

Hutchinson, (a division of Random House Publishing Group Ltd), Random House, 20 Vauxhall Bridge Road, London, SW1V 2SA.

Michael Joseph Ltd, (a division of Penguin Books Ltd), 27 Wrights Lane, London, W8 5TZ.

Arc Publications, The Nanholme Centre, Shaw Wood Road, Todmorden, Lancashire, OL14 6DA.

Oxford University Press, Walton Street, Oxford, OX2 6DP

Peterloo Poets, 2 Kelly Gardens, Calstock, Cornwall, PH8 9SA.

Polygon Press, 90 Edinburgh's University Press, 22 George Street, Edinburgh, EH8 9LF.

Robson Books Ltd, Bolsover House, 5-6 Clipstone Street, London, W1P 7EB.

Sinclair-Stevenson, (a division of Reed International Books), Michelin House, 81 Fulham Road, London, SW3 6RB.

Secker & Warburg, (a division of Reed International Books), Michael House, 81 Fulham Road, London, SW3 6RB.

Seren Books, (an imprint of Poetry Wales Press), First Floor, 2 Wyndham Street, Bridgend, Mid Glamorgan, CF31 1EF.

Virago Press, Centro House, 20-23 Mandela Street, London, NW1 0HQ.

The Women's Press, 34 Great Sutton Street, London, EC1V 0DX.

Chapter Twelve

Small Presses — The Final Frontier

And having failed as a commercial proposition, been turned down by the specialists or found them lacking, what next? Is the mainstream everything? For some poets the accolade bestowed by a major publisher's colophon on their volume is worth almost as much as having the poems published in the first place. John Ormond, who lived his life in pursuit of excellence, regarded the publication of his *Definition Of A Waterfall* by the prestigious Oxford University Press as a justifiable acknowledgement of his talent. By contrast John Tripp, who, along with John Ormond and Emyr Humphreys, made up the famous Anglo-Welsh Volume 27 of Penguin's *Modern Poets* series, was content to blast at the world from the side trenches of a whole series of small publishers ranging from Tony Curtis' Edge Press to my own Second Aeon.

One of the great joys of poetry publishing is that its proliferation never ends. Beyond the mainstream lie the alternatives, the non-commercial opposers of centralism, the independents, the pamphleteers, the politically correct, the 'small is beautifuls', the freaks, the loonies, the provocateurs, the sideshows, the hobbyists, the recherché literateurs, the obtuse, the reclusive, the printer artists and the self-publishers. All working to bring out their books of poems and, for one of a hundred reasons, to release them on the wider world.

Most imitate the commercial market leaders, at least as far as they are able. Forest Books look for all the world like Bloodaxe Books; Swansea Poetry Workshop publications thoroughly resemble the products of Seren and Poetry Wales Press. Others take a joy in avoiding the system altogether, making non-conformity their raison d'être. Sound poet Bob Cobbing's Writers Forum has by now brought out more than 500 publications. His output includes literary best-sellers from Eric Mottram, Allen Ginsberg and Jeff Nuttall, although much of his output is so fugitive as to appear almost invisible. Single cards in envelopes printed in editions of 50, hand-sized mini-books which vanish at their poetry reading launches, untraceable booklets with no imprint publication data. Who exactly was it, who published

Jack Kerouac's *Old Angel Midnight?* The library system cannot cope and gives up. Collectors fruitlessly track such publications through networks of specialist shops and backstreet dealers. It's a William Burroughs world of cut-ups, slow shuffles, paste-in and invading Martians. If the British Government had really wanted to keep Peter Wright silent they should have arranged for him to be published by Cobbing. The style is the fulcrum of Writer's Forum's view of culture: a centralist literature run by an inner circle, which is best opposed not by confrontation (although Bob has tried that), but by the establishment of a genuine alternative. Some works do have legible titles, addresses and prices, and thanks to Cobbing's dynamic photocopier nothing ever goes o.p. — Connie Sirr's *A Further Choice of Whiskies* (found texts), Betty Radin's *Dancing Through The Streets*, Patrick Fetherston's *Noons And Afternoons,* Nicholas Johnson's *Eel Earth,* and Geraldine Monk's amazing *Quaquauersals.* And amazing stuff it is, too. A selection from the whole range appears in the anthology *Verbivisivoco — A Performance of Poetry.* Send to 89a Petherton Road, London, N5 2QT, and hope.

The British Library calls this kind of activity 'Grey Publishing', although when they established the term they had in mind the products of those who are not normally publishers at all — local authorities, boards, trusts — rather than the works of those out to subvert the system.

It would be stretching credibility to claim that most small publishers have revolution at the top of their agendas. The vast majority are content to remain genuine alternatives to the commercial process. Their two trade associations, the older and more creatively minded Association of Little Presses (founded in 1966) and the brasher Small Press Group (founded 1989) both run bookfairs, publish catalogues and give off an air of non-corporate vigour.

The SPG's hirsute chairman, John Nicholson, remarks in his introduction to their Yearbook that one of the intentions of the SPG is to "refute the notion that publishing is a world peopled by tycoons, poseurs and other assorted empty-headed flunkies. It is commonplace to argue that the establishment presses and institutions are desperate to preserve a stranglehold on ideas, opinion, information and culture in general". The little publishers threaten them. SPG small presses go in for the kill.

At the ALP, Robert Sheppard is keen to dispel any idea that small presses only ever bring out 'division two' poets: "the best of the little presses have often transcended this notion by defining what poetry will be, by publishing work which breaks conventional paradigms of what poetry has been; in other words, by publishing work which, to the trained eyes of commercial poetry editors, appears not to be poetry at all".(*ALP Catalogue of Little Press Books in Print*).

Who ends up defining just what late twentieth century poetry is, then? The editors? The readers? Or the poets? The answer depends on who you ask.

In terms of circulation battles, commerce wins hands down with its recognised bestsellers. No little press is ever going to match Faber and Faber with its sales of Larkin, Hughes or Heaney. Yet when you get down among the lesser-knowns, the competition becomes more even. Little difference can be discerned between the print runs for (say) Secker and Warburg's John Burnside set *Common Knowledge* and (say) North and South's *Rope Boy To The Rescue* by Lee Harwood. Secker get there by spreading copies in parcels of two or three in bookshops throughout the UK; North and South sell via the author, direct to readers and to the specialists.

A very high percentage of small publishing turns out to be creative writing with more than fifty per cent of that poetry. Novelists, biographers, and cook-book writers may occasionally go it alone, but really they need the commercial structure in order to succeed. Poets, however, can always get where they want by alternative routes.

To survey the UK's total small press output in one briefish overlook is obviously an impossibility. Instead I have chosen, almost at random, a number of representative activists of differing kinds. Readers keen to learn more are advised to write to the presses themselves — much useful information can be garnered from the directories published by both the ALP and the SPG. Write to them at: Association of Little Presses, c/o 89a Petherton Road, London, N5 2QT and Small Press Group at Middlesex University, White Hart Lane, London, N17 3HR. Check Appendix VI, which lists addresses for some of the main operators.

Peter Mortimer's Iron Press produces editions well up to commercial standard; indeed, barring the use of coloured endpapers, it is difficult to tell them and Bloodaxe Books apart. Like many small publishing operations, Mortimer's revolves around his well established North-Eastern journal of poetry and fiction, *Iron*, now more than twenty years old. Magazines often do this to editors: they suggest gaps in the market and then fill them with appropriate contributors, the editors suddenly finding themselves well into book publishing without exerting any conscious effort of will. Mortimer's operation throws up at least three titles annually — a book of fiction, a collection of poems and perhaps an anthology is average. *Iron's* current catalogue lists 30 titles, most expected Geordie fare, but with a few surprises. One, their very successful anthology *The Poetry of Perestroika*, collects the work of some 30 Soviet poets writing with the reins loosened. These excellent translations by Carol Rumens and company make this an exciting find. Mortimer has already shifted more than a 1000 copies. A mini book that has sold even more (2500 at last count), is *The Haiku Hundred*, produced in co-operation with the British Haiku Society. Poets on the *Iron* list include Charles Wilkinson, Moira Andrew, Raymond Tallis and Joe Smythe — curiously none of them from the North East. Mortimer politely points out that *Iron* does not actively seek book manuscripts and suggests that poets try the magazine first.

Someone once called Huddersfield "the poetry capital of Britain", and Peter Sansom at The Poetry Business has been exploiting this ever since. Like Peter Mortimer, he began with a magazine, *The North*, which subsequently expanded to include the publication of books. Sansom gives his all to poetry — he's a fine writer himself, with a Carcanet book to his credit — and along with Janet Fisher runs an advice, criticism, and information bureau in rooms above a Victorian arcade in Huddersfield. There they also find time to publish Smith/Doorstop Books. Starting with a double header pamphlet by Clare Chapman and Simon Armitage back in 1986, he is now bringing out between four and five titles annually, usually in editions of 300 to 500. The range encompasses Ian MacMillan, Martyn Wiley, Geoff Hattersley, David Annwn, Sue Dymoke, Paul Matthews, Owen Davis, Michael Farley, Anna Fissler and many others. Over the years, production standards have risen sharply. Both *Ghosts of A Chance* by John Harvey and *Opening The Ice* by Ann Dancy and Myra Schneider are printed offset, and well up to Bloodaxe standard. A recent departure is a series of full length poetry cassettes with Ian MacMillan, Carol Ann Duffy, Sujata Bhatt and Simon Armitage tight and neat in plastic boxes. Sansom and Fisher are "actively seeking manuscripts", but do buy a few of their productions before blazing in.

Stride, which is probably the best known and the widest distributed of the alternative presses, is again an outgrowth of a periodical — the infamous *Stride* magazine, which embraced the entire little mag world like a punk predator during its early 80s heyday. Editor Rupert Loydell has long since abandoned the little mag wars to concentrate on book production and, by dint of buying up Michael Farley's ailing Taxus imprint and sheer hard slog now boasts a stock list of more than 100 titles. In terms of content, Stride treads the fringes with forays into the middle. Long happy to produce books and booklets by Chris Bendon, David Caddy, Brian Louis Pearce, Martin Hibbert, Len Mullan and other stalwarts of the small mag scene, Stride has steadily been showing increasing amounts of creative muscle with titles by Rosalind Brackenbury, Jay Ramsay, Peter Redgrove, David Miller and Andrew Jordan. There are anthologies of women's writing, American poetry, work from the inner cities, spiritual verse and *Ladder To The Next Floor*, a huge collection of the best of the magazine published in association with the University of Salzburg. Loydell declares an interest in "the experimentation/style/content of 'the small presses' [meaning presumably the radical ones] but not in their presentation". His stock list is as catholic as one could want. Production remains down the line a little but it is improving fast. Password distribution gets it around the country and bestsellers include Peter Redgrove's *Dressed As for A Tarot Pack* and a quite original anthology of New Wave poets writing for children, *The Bees Knees*. There is no denying the energy at work here.

By total contrast Alex Crossley aims to take the poetry world by stealth with his Lymes Press, producing classy, if unadventurous-looking 200 copy letterpress pamphlets of nineteenth century French verse, seventeenth century English verse and compilations of Anglo-Italian post-war poetry. Latest title is *The Life And Selected Writings of Richard Barnfield — 1574-1627*. Crossley hunts always "for something of interest which might have enough appeal to subsidize other more avant-garde texts". How successful is he? Much depends, I suppose, on how you define the cutting edge.

Roland John, at Hippopotamus Press, has done things in reverse of usual order. He founded his Press in 1973 in order to "publish first collections...by those we feel are unfashionable or unfairly neglected" and only much later took on a magazine, in his case *Outposts* following the death of Howard Sergeant. Unlike Sergeant's seemingly endless booklet series of works by unknowns which accompanied the magazine, Hippopotamus has no truck whatsoever with vanity. Titles are entirely Roland John and his partner B.A. Martin's choice: middle mainstream, well-crafted, unflashy works of worth

— Shaun McCarthy, Humphrey Clucas, Lotte Kramer, Peter Dent and Hippo's greatest discovery Debjani Chatterjee. Bestsellers include Edward Lowbury's *Selected and New Poems* and Peter Dent's *Distant Lamps*. Like many presses Hippopotamus began with pamphlets and by now produces hardbacks well up to trade standard. No home for the experimental, but rather, like Enitharmon, has a good feel for the cultured and the neglected.

The slick sounding A Twist In the Tail, run by Paul Cookson, was established in 1980, for the by now familiar reason of getting the operator's own poetry into print. Cookson, then making a name for himself on the performance poetry circuit ("more versatile than Batman's utility belt"), needed a book quickly. The venture worked and he soon found himself publishing fellow performers like Kev Fegan, Ian Macmillan, Martyn Wiley and Henry Normal. With the latter he established The Amazing Colossal Press, another outlet for performers, now run by Maureen Richardson. In the past five years Cookson reckons to have moved some 10,000 units, not at all impossible for a writer dedicated to broad audiences. My excellently printed and very non-little press looking sample copies of *The Toilet Seat Has Teeth!* and *Spill The Beans* both came ready autographed and with a bit of pushing managed to raise a laugh.

The neatly named Reality Street Editions was formed in 1993 by the amalgamation of Wendy Mulford's Cambridge Street Editions with Ken Edwards' London Reality Studios. The press is the nearest the UK has to a L=A=N=G=U=A=G=E poetry publisher, producing distinctive editions, "innovative and challenging", from verse's outer edge. Typical writers include Kelvin Corcoran, Maggie O'Sullivan, Denise Riley and Allen Fisher. Just as cultured as Enitharmon, as controlled as Peterloo, as wild as Writers Forum. The face British poetry small presses were built for.

The editors of *Agenda* magazine, one of the longer-lived UK poetry journals, found, like almost everyone else involved in the literary magazine game, that a quarterly compilation is often not enough. Agenda Editions, published by the team of William Cookson and Peter Dale, are workmanlike books looking for all the world like special issues of the magazine from which they sprang. Cookson's taste comes from his early interest in David Jones, Peter Russell and Ezra Pound, all of whom he met. In fact it was Pound himself who ghost-wrote the editorial to Agenda's first issue, wanting to name the mag *Four Pages* as a continuation of a periodical he had once instigated. Over the years, *Agenda* has produced much sought-after books, both of original works and of criticism by and about this group of writers. The compass later expanded to include Basil Bunting, Robert Lowell and Geoffrey Hill. Recent editions include Anne Beresford's *The Self of the Morning*, co-published with Turret Books, and Desmond O'Grady's *Seven Arab Odes*.

In West Wales Anne Lewis-Smith, who edited *Envoi* magazine for years before passing it on to Roger Elkin, now concentrates on Envoi Poets Publications, producing a steady stream of pamphlets by new writers: 90 since the press's establishment in 1985 with more still on the way. Design is non-existent, as for the most part is any real concept of marketing. Titles are subsidised almost entirely by their authors. Anne Lewis-Smith tells me that she feels "very strongly that there comes a certain period in a poet's development when they need a wider platform than small magazines", and here she is absolutely correct. Money might change hands during the production of Envoi publications but profit, if there ever is any, goes back to the poet. Typical titles include Alistair Halden's *To Travel Hopefully*, Hugh McMillan's *Triumph of The Air*, Jennifer Footman's *Through A Stained Glass Window* and Mary Hodgson's *New World*. It is hardly ground-shaking material, rather the product of steady hands. Anne Lewis Smith is calling a halt at book number 100, "being nearer 70 than 60", as she puts it, she wants to concentrate on her own writing.

Brenda Walker's Forest Books perhaps should be included among the UK's semi-commercial poetry specialists. Her approach is totally professional. Forest, which began in 1984 as a hobby, specialises in English verse translations of international poetry across the broadest of fronts with a particular emphasis on minorities. The back list is nothing short of enormous and includes works from as wildly different cultures as those of Sri Lanka, Taiwan, Ireland and Iran. The largest part, though, concentrates on Eastern Europe. By 1988 production had reached a high enough level to free Brenda Walker from full time teaching and enable her to devote more time to poetry. Revelling in the description 'cultural adventurer' she now tours embassies, foundations, ministries of culture and the like, raising the necessary cash to fund her excellently produced volumes. With thirteen new titles and seven or so reprints each year this can be quite a task. Typical titles include *An Elusive Eagle Soars* — modern Albanian poetry, *Lifting The Stone* — Jewish mythic work from Jason Sommer, *Reddened Water Flows Clear* by Sri Lankan Jean Arasanayagam, *Faint Shadows of Love* by Korean Kwang-kyu Kim and *In Celebration of Mihai Eminescu*, the work of Romania's National Poet translated by Brenda Walker herself. There is a large catalogue available.

Robert Richardson's The Big Little Poem Series began in 1982 as a series of finely printed poem postcards mostly dedicated to "the imagist principle of precise language" and contemporary approaches to the lyric and epigram. Centrepiece of the press's activity has been the 1989 *Homage To Imagism* series of events put on to celebrate the movement which, in 1909 Paris, initiated one of Modernism's great literary revolutions. Richardson's card series, well funded by the local arts association, includes Roland John, William Cookson, Peter Dent, Joy Thorpe, Malcolm Carson, Keith Bosley and others. The association with some of the *Agenda* team has lead to a few fine booklets, notably A *Set of Darts — Epigrams for the Nineties* and Ondra Lysohorsky's *The White Raven and other poems*. One gets the feeling of style, erudition and sly jokiness here. Authors are usually invited although unsolicited contributions are not unacceptable. As an offshoot Richardson has taken on board the inimitable French concretist Henri Chopin and established Concrete Events, a further postcard series. These are far less successful to my mind, appearing to be somewhat stuck in the 60s and without the anarchic lift of Cobbing nor the class of Ian Hamilton Finlay. But it is a field in which few work today.

Prest Roots Press was set up by Peter Larkin "to bring together innovative poetry and find tradional printing at affordable prices". His special interest is 'Cambridge' poetry, minimalist, pastoral work of the Paul Green, John Wilkinson, Ian Hamilton Finlay, Thomas A. Clark and J.H. Prynne variety. These last three provide his best sellers. The editons have class, and low circulations (150 copies is typical). Larkin has brought out his own *Pastoral Advert* as part of the series, a large format, letterpress, sewn edition that is a delight both to read and handle. He claims that his "low-consumer life-style" has enable him to give practical help to his publishing projects. I hope he keeps it up.

Allardyce, Barnett was for a time the Cambridge group's main publisher, producing large collected volumes by the group's prime movers: Douglas Oliver, Andrew Crozier, J.H. Prynne and Anthony Barnett himself. There was a magazine too, *Poetica*, devoted to the kind of post-modernism most other editors leave out. But the advent of the (now defunct) Paladin imprint at Grafton and the departure of a number of key authors has left things somewhat in disarray. Barnett, however, is not a man to be stopped. His recent 'acts of defiance' have been volumes by Andrea Zanzotto (translated from the Italian), Anne-Marie Albiach (from the French), plus a new one by himself. These are slim, traditional productions which belie their innovative content and give the poetry world a lot of hope.

The KQBX Press was formed in Bournemouth a decade ago by John Selby, Keith Selby and James Sale to publish cheap, photocopied, staplebound booklets of poetry from the southern region. Over the years aid from Southern Arts and from the local council have enabled the press to vastly improve their slim volume production standards. Taste is towards the traditional, which has given the operation some impressive sales figures. Typical poets include David Orme, Sarah Hopkins, David Caddy and Anthony Watts. Flambard Press, run from the northeast by Welshman Peter Elfed Lewis, is of more recent origin. Flambard's policy is to work on a personal basis with local poets "unlikely to interest a commercial house in London or elsewhere". So far Cynthia Fuller, Andrea Capes and Christopher Pilling have benefited, but Northern Arts support will enable Lewis to increase his range. Production is of the neatest I've seen. *Slow Dancer*, one of the best ever British magazines may have limboed into the sunset, but John Harvey's eclectic vision lives on with Slow Dancer Press. "Poetry is something that is alive and many-sided and defies boundaries and rules — a slithering, bouyant living thing. Just when you think you've caught it — there it's gone." Harvey's slow editions range from pamphlets to spine-bound books; from unknowns like Rhoda McAdam to top of the tree works like Lee Harwood's *In The Mists*.

Aloes Books, run by Jim Pennington, is a sporadic publisher of poetry and fiction with a distinctly 70s Thomas Pynchon/Lou Reed/Jeff Nuttall feel. Access to occasional funding has given output an uneven look. Their bestsellers, New York performance poet Max Blagg's *Licking The Fun Up* and Jeff Nuttall's *What Happened To Jackson* are both glossy jobs, while Colin Simms' *Flat Earth* is a typical small press production. Other authors include Patti Smith, Larry Eigner and Kathy Acker. Highly collectable stuff.

Frustration with the system doesn't have to mean poor production standards. North and South, founded in 1986 to bring out David Annwn's *King Saturn's Book*, rejected by everyone else, manages some of the nicest looking volumes in the business. Run by Peterjon and Yasmin Skelt the operation publishes one or two titles annually, usually by poets from the *Paladin New British Poetry Anthology*. Typical are Lee Harwood, Eric Mottram, Richard Caddel, Frances Presley, Elaine Randell (rejected everywhere else as "too depressing") and Kelvin Corcoran. Catalogue available.

Occasionally non-poetry presses fall into publishing verse. Local history publisher, The Rockingham Press, run by former radio producer David Perman, has just launched a poetry list with Feyyaz Fergar's *A Talent For Shrouds*, English language works written by one of Turkey's contemporary lights, and followed it with books by William Oxley, Chris Bendon and Mercer Simpson's illustrated *East Anglian Wordscapes*. Not the usual route, but then that's what small presses are known for.

Ending nearer home, Chris Mills' Red Sharks Press was not an outgrowth of a magazine (no matter how much Mills has tried to involve himself in that field of endeavour), nor was it primarily a vehicle to bring the works of C. Mills before the general public, although it has done this with considerable aplomb: *Rumour Mathematics*, *The Bicycle Is An Easy Pancake* and more recently the definitive Mills, *The Dancing Drayman*. Red Sharks began as an outgrowth of local poetry activity in Cardiff, notably the Cabaret 246 performance group which, for a brief time, united writers from a considerable range of backgrounds, and more recently Undercover Writers, an open city-centre one-stop for poets, fiction writers and critics. Once started Mills found he couldn't stop. He became everybody's archetypical small press publisher: no helpers, no grants to start with although he has one now, a handbuilder of his own publications, spine-bound with the aid of bricks and with stuck-on postcard covers, a rearranger of bookshop displays, forever to be found flogging his works outside readings and literary events. Since 1983, when he began, he has managed more than 50 publications and still feels that any minute now things could "go big". He pushes his local circle with zeal — Jackie Aplin's *Kissing's For Cissies*, Susan Mann's *I'm Always Put Off My Food When It Snores*, Laura Barnes' *Still Have Sex*, Richard Gwyn's *Defying Gravity* — although he is not averse to publishing from further away, notably Ian MacMillan and Geoff Hattersley. His greatest success has been Ifor Thomas, who has shifted upwards of 1500 copies of his *Giving Blood* series. "A good local poetry scene with good advice from some old hands has been positively life saving at times", comments Mills. And I'm sure he'll continue.

APPENDIX I
Books for the Poet

A: Some Anthologies

One of the simplest ways of discovering the full range of contemporary verse is to read a few anthologies. Those in the following list, which is by no means definitive, are mostly in print and should be available through good bookshops or in cases of difficulty from one of the specialist shops listed in Appendix II. How do you improve your ability to write? First you read the work of others.

The Rattle Bag edited by Seamus Heaney and Ted Hughes, Faber and Faber, 1982. Designed originally as a new introduction to poetry for young people this splendid and seemingly arbitary selection of verse from all over, arranged alphabetically by title and for the most part avoiding standard anthology texts, turns out to be the best single volume introduction around. Mainly, but not exclusively, twentieth century — wide ranging, big, paperbacked, and cheap.

The Forward Book Of Poetry published annually by Faber and Faber in association with Forward Publishing and launched on National Poetry Day. A selection of the best contemporary poetry published in Britain last year, compiled as part of the William Sieghart's Forward Poetry prize. Serves as a readable map to recent activity.

The New Poetry edited by Micheal Hulse, David Kennedy, David Morley, Bloodaxe Books, 1993. The controversial anthology of new British and Irish poets of the 80s and 90s. Amazing omissions and incredible inclusions aside, this set has at least been drawn from a thorough trawl of both major and minor publishers and a look at most poets operating in these islands today.

The New British Poetry 1968-88 edited by Gillian Allnutt, Fred D'Aguiar, Ken Edwards and Eric Mottram, Paladin, 1988. Poetry of the fringes, the minorities and the under-represented. Divided into four sections — younger, older, black and women — this one is often as exciting as anything else around.

Grandchildren Of Albion edited by Michael Horovitz, New Departures, 1992. An illustrated anthology of voices and visions of younger poets in Britain. Performers, rappers, pop singers — the whole mainstream alternative in one large go.

The Popular Front Of Contemporary Poetry edited by Paul Beasley, Apples and Snakes, 1992. British performance poetry.

Hearsay edited by Paul Beasley, Bodley Head, 1994. Performance poetry. (Cassette available from 57 Productions.)

Verbi Visi Voco edited by Bob Cobbing and Bill Griffiths, Writers Forum, 1992. Sound, visual, concrete and experimental poetry from the past twenty years.

The Penguin Book of Contemporary British Poetry edited by Blake Morrison and Andrew Motion, Penguin, 1982. How the poetry world looked a decade ago, a highly biased and very selective anthology which nonetheless has a fair number of high spots.

The New Poetry edited by A. Alvarez, Penguin, 1962. British poets who came into their own during the 50s.

British Poetry Since 1945 edited by Edward Lucie Smith, Penguin, 1970, revised 1985. An overview of the whole academic vs modernist world of post war British verse.

The Oxford Book Of Contemporary Verse 1945-1980 edited by D.J. Enright, Oxford University Press, 1980. Forty British, American and Commonwealth poets who have emerged since the war.

The Faber Book Of Contemporary American Poetry edited by Helen Vendler, Faber and Faber, 1986. Thirty-five poets in generous selections, described as "discriminating" but still worth reading.

The Penguin Book Of American Verse edited by Geoffrey Moore, Penguin, 1977, revised 1989. A broad sweep from seventeeth-century beginnings to the present.

The Faber Book Of Modern European Poetry edited by A. Alvarez, Faber and Faber, 1992. Thirty poets in verse translation. From traditions of increasing influence on British verse.

Child Of Europe: A New Anthology Of East European Poetry edited by Michael March, Penguin, 1990. Now that the wall has come down, a welcome overview.

The Bright Field edited by Meic Stephens, Carcanet, 1991. Contemporary Welsh poets writing in English with generous selections by the individual poets concerned.

Poetry Wales: 25 Years edited by Cary Archard, Seren, 1990. A broad ranging selection from Wales' premier poetry magazine.

The Bloodaxe Book Of Contemporary Women Poets edited by Jeni Couzyn, Bloodaxe, 1985. Large selections by eleven British women poets.

The Faber Book of 20th Century Women's Poetry edited by Fleur Adcock, Faber and Faber, 1987. A broader overview.

New Women Poets edited by Carol Rumens, Bloodaxe, 1990. Twenty-five new voices.

Sixty Women Poets edited by Linda France, Bloodaxe, 1994. The last two decades in Britain and Ireland.

News For Babylon edited by James Berry, Chatto and Windus, 1984. West Indian-British poetry in large selection.

In The American Tree edited by Ron Silliman, National Poetry Foundation Inc., 1986. Full blown language poetry anthology, anathema to some, all there is to others.

Post-modern American Poetry edited by Paul Hoover, Norton, 1994. Wonderful selection of US alternatives from Ginsberg to Coolidge.

B: Reference Books

The Poet's Manual and Rhyming Dictionary by Frances Stillman, Thames and Hudson, 1966. Extensive and compactly arranged rhyme dictionary plus complete introduction to the various metres, stanzas and poetic forms used in English verse.

The Penguin Rhyming Dictionary by Rosalind Fergusson, Penguin, 1985. Comprehensive computer-prepared dictionary based on phonetic principles. When stuck for a rhyme don't be afraid to consult volumes like these. Established poets make use of them all the time.

The Princeton Encyclopedia of Poetry and Poetics edited by Alex Preminger, Macmillan, 1974. A thoroughly browsable compendium of over 1000 entries covering everything from cinquains to sentimentality, taking in medieval romance, chants, charm, limericks and obscurity en route.

C: *Guides*

Poetry Handbook For Readers And Writers by Dinah Livingstone, Macmillan, 1993. Compact tour of poetry mechanics, covering sound, shape, content, poetry in society, translation and performance.

The Poet's Handbook by Judson Jermone, Writer's Digest Books, 1980. American guide to metrics taken at a steady pace.

The Way To Write Poetry by Michael Baldwin, Elm Tree Books, 1982. Serious, basic advice for beginners.

The Craft Of Writing Poetry by Allison Chilsholm, Allison and Busby, 1992. Practical introduction for beginners.

The Art Of Writing Poetry by Allison Chilsholm, Writers College, 1993. Correspondence course available from Sevendale House, 7 Dale Street, Manchester, M1 1JB.

Writing Poems by Peter Sansom, Bloodaxe, 1993. Best single volume on the subject from the man who runs the original "Poetry Business" in Huddersfield.

How to Publish Your Poetry by Peter Finch, Allison and Busby, 1985, revised 1991. Complete guide to the poetry world from preparation of manuscripts to public readings taking in self publication, rejection and copyright on the way.

Getting Into Poetry by Paul Hyland, Bloodaxe, 1992. A readers' and writers' guide to the poetry scene including extensive reading lists.

How to Enjoy Poetry by Vernon Scannell, Piatkus, 1983. What is it? How do you appreciate it? With essays on the craft of writing, poetry's changing face and contemporary looks.

How to Speak A Poem by Betty Mulcahy, Autolycus Press, 1987. Handbook for reciters, speakers and performers.

How Poetry Works, by Philip Davies Roberts, Penguin, 1986. The poem on the page vs the poem on the ear. A comprehensive introduction to the whole art and one of the best available.

How to Study Modern Poetry by Tony Curtis, Macmillan, 1990. How to come to terms with modern poetry and cope with work which does not seem part of a tradition and does not seem to rhyme or scan.

Studying Poetry by R.T. Jones, Edward Arnold, 1986. A terse, jargon-free introduction to how poetry works.

Poetry In English by Charles Barber, Macmillan, 1983. An introduction to poetry in the English language from Chaucer to the present day.

Poetry Listing by David Hart. A five volume survey of the whole scene detailing everything from New Zealand small presses to mainstream American masterworks. Volume five, the last in the series, also contains interviews with leading practitioners. Best map there is. Available directly from Wood Wind Publications, 42 All Saints Road, Kings Heath, Birmingham, B14 7LL.

APPENDIX II
Bookshops

With the exception of a core stock of anthologies and the selected output of major commercial houses, and despite the New Generation Poetry boom hype, poetry still does not sell too well in the high street, certainly not well enough to justify permanent prominent bookshop space. The town centre independent will have half a shelf, W.H. Smith might manage a whole one. Ted Hughes, Roger McGough, some Faber darlings, Helen Steiner Rice. Customers in reach of a Waterstones or a Dillons will fare much better. To a certain extent these stores believe in literature but even so the real poetry fan will be left wanting. Where do you get the products of the small presses? The range of titles put out by the specialists and the independents? And for an even harder search just where in the UK do you buy a selection of small magazines? Some of the following shops may help, all deal by mail order. For a fuller list check with *The Poetry Library* at the Royal Festival Hall, South Bank Centre, London, SE1 8XX (tel: 071 921 0664) who publish a regular update.

Alan Halsey / The Poetry Bookshop, West House, Broad Street, Hay-on-Wye, HR3 5DB. Tel: 0497 820 305.

Bernard Stone / The Turret Bookshop, 36 Great Queen Street, London, WC2B 5AA. Tel: 071 831 5789. One of the all time great poetry bookshops.

Blackwells, Broad Street, Oxford, OX1 3BQ. Tel: 0865 792792.

The Book Case, 29 Market Street, Hebden Bridge, West Yorks, HX7 6EU. Tel: 0422 844295.

The Book Shop, 20 High Street, Princes Risborough, Bucks, HP27 0AX.

Cactus Bookshop, 2b Hope Street, Hanley, Stoke on Trent, ST1 5BS. Tel: 0782 204449.

Compendium Books, 234 Camden High Street, London, NW1. Tel: 071 267 1525.

Four Provinces Bookshop (specialists in Irish poetry), 244 Grays Inn Road, London, WC1X 8JR. Tel: 071 833 3022.

Frontline Books, 1 Newton Street, Piccadilly, Manchester, M1 1HW.

Gateway Paperbacks, Chester Street, Shrewsbury, SY1 1NB. Tel: 0743 355109.

Green Ink Bookshop (specialists in Irish poetry), 8 Archway Mall London, N19 5RG. Tel: 071 263 4748.

Hazeldene Bookshop, 61 Renshaw Street, Liverpool, L1 2SJ. Tel: 051 708 8780.

Heffers Booksellers, 20 Trinity Street, Cambridge, CB2 3NG. Tel: 0223 358351.

Iain Sinclair, (mail order only), 28 Albion Drive, London, E8 4ET. Tel: 071 254 8571.

Lamp Community Bookshop, 91 Bradshawgate, Leigh, Lancashire, WN7 4ND. Tel: 0942 606667.

Mushroom Books, 10 Heathcote Street, Nottingham, NG1 3AA. Tel: 0602 582506.

Oriel, The Friary, Cardiff, CF1 4AA. Tel: 0222 395548.

Owl Bookshop, 211 Kentish Town Road, London, NW5. Tel: 071 485 7793.

Paul Green, 83b London Road, Peterborough, Cambs. Mail order only.

Peter Riley, 27 Sturton Street, Cambridge, CB1 2QC. Tel: 0223 327455. Visitors by appointment only. Stocks mainly second hand, small press and imported items.

Public House Bookshop, 21 Little Preston Street, Brighton, BN1 2HQ. Tel: 0273 328357.

Silver Moon Women's Bookshop, 64-68 Charing Cross Road, London, WC2H 0BB. Tel: 071 379 1018.

Trinity Books, 2 Trinity Gardens, New Church Lane, Ulverston, Cumbria, LA12 7UB. Tel: 0229 580346. Second hand and small press items. Deals by post.

The Wall Bookshop, St Mary at the Wall, Church Street, Colchester. Tel: 0206 577301.

APPENDIX III
Some Poetry Competions

A selective list of poetry competitions during the two years preceeding this book's compilation. Prospective entrants are advised to send the organisers a stamped addressed envelope and a request for fuller details of the contest *before* sending any poetry in. Competitions do not necessarily repeat annually and the details of prizes and judges here are typical and not definitive. Closing dates change. Organisers give up. Check first. A fuller list is available from the Poetry Library, Royal Festival Hall, South Bank Centre, London, SE1 8XX. Tel: 071 921 0664/0943.

Afan Poetry Society Competition — 74 Wildbrook, Taibach, West Glamorgan, SA13 2UN. First prize: £75. Judges: Sally Roberts Jones, Alan Davies.

Arvon International Poetry Competition — Kilnhurst, Kilnhurst Road, Todmorden, Lancashire, OL14 6AX. First prize: £5000. Judges: Eavan Boland, Gillian Clarke, Liz Lochhead, Penelope Shuttle.

Bamford Memorial Trophy Competition — Gary Couzens, Flat 2, 123 St Michael's Road, Aldershot, Hants, GU12 4JW. First prize: £50. Judge: Martyn Crucefix.

Blue Nose Poets-of-the-Year Competition — 72 First Avenue, Bush Hill Park, Enfield, Middlesex, EN1 1BW. First prize: more than £10. Judges: Martyn Crucefix, Mario Petrucci and Sue Hubbard.

Bournemouth International Festival Open Poetry Competition — Suite 2, Digby Chambers, Post Office Road, Bournemouth, Dorset, BH1 1BA. First prize: £200. Judge: Hilary Davies.

Bridport Arts Centre Creative Writing Competition — 9 Pier Terrace, West Bay, Bridport, Dorset, DT6 4ER. First prize: £1000. Judges: Brian McCabe, Lawrence Sail.

Capricorn International Poetry Competition — 17 West Lea Road, Bath, BA1 3RL. First prize: £100.

City of Cardiff International Poetry Competition — PO Box 438, Cardiff, CF1 6YA. First prize: £1000. Judges: Moniza Alvi, Leslie Norris.

Chiltern Writers Group Creative Writing Competition (Poetry Section) — Edith Crisp, 116 Wendover Road, Weston Turville, Aylesbury,

Bucks, HP22 5TE. First prize: £50. Judges: Frances Wilson and Elizabeth Buchan.

Co-Operative Retail Services Caring Poetry Festival — 29 Danzic Street, Manchester, M4 4BA. Entries possible in any British or ethnic community language.

Dragonheart Press Poetry Competition — 11 Menin Road, Allestree, Derby, DE22 2NL. First prize: publication in book form. Judges: Press editors.

Dulwich Festival Poetry Competition — Wendy French, 4 Myton Road, West Dulwich, London, SE21 8EB. First prize: £150. Judge: Wendy Cope.

English Explorer Magazine National Poetry Competition — Warwick House, Station Approach, Dorridge, Solihull, West Midlands, B93 8JA. First prize: £500. Judges: board of editors.

Envoi International Poetry Competition — David Bowes, 17 Millcroft, Bishop's Stortford, Herts, CM23 2BP. First prize: £100. Judge: Tony Sims.

Exile Poetry Competition — 38 Emerald Street, Saltburn by the Sea, Cleveland, TS12 1ED. First prize: £10. Judge: *Exile* magazine editors.

Friends of Dog Watch Open Poetry Competition — 267 Milbury Road, Warlingham, Surrey, CR6 9TL. First prize: £25. Judges: *Dog Watch Newsletter* editors.

Forward Prizes for Poetry — in addition to £10,000 annually for the best published collection and £5000 for the best *first* collection there is a now a new award of £1000 for the best poem, published, but not yet actually part of a collection. Write to Sandra Vince, Prize Administrator, Book Trust, Book House, 45 East Hill, London, SW18 2QZ.

Frogmore Poetry Prize — 42 Moreehall Avenue, Folkestone, Kent. First prize: 100 guineas plus a life subscription to the magazine *Frogmore papers*. Judge: Pauline Stainer.

Glengettie Tea John Tripp Award For Spoken Poetry — The Welsh Academy, Third Floor, Mount Stuart House, Mount Stuart Square, Cardiff, CF1 6DQ. First prize: £1000. Judges: Robin Reeves, Adrian Henri, Peter Finch.

Helena Poetry Circle Open Poetry Competition — Corner House, High St, Newport, Saffron Walden, Essex, CB11 3QX. First prize: £250. Judge: Richard Burns.

Kent & Sussex Open Poetry Competition — John Arnold, 39 Rockingham Way, Crowborough, East Sussex, TN6 2NJ. First prize: £300. Judge: E.A. Markham

Kitley Trust Poetry Competition — 8 Oakbrook Road, Sheffield, S11 7EA. First prize: £40. Judge: Neil Astley.

Lace Open Poetry Competition — The Day Centre, Park Street, Lincoln, LN1 1UQ. First prize: £200. Judge: Alan Brownjohn.

Lancaster Literature Festival National Poetry Competition — LitFest Office, 67 Church Street, Lancaster, LA1 1ET. Prizes include publication, readings plus £20. Judges: Robert Minhinnick, Jo Shapcott.

Library of Avalon Poetry Competition — The Ark, The Glastonbury Experience, 2-4 High St., Glastonbury, Somerset, BA6 9DU. First prize: £100. Judges: Geoffrey Ashe, Rose Flint and others.

Lincolnshire Literature Festival National Poetry Competition — L.L.F., The Word Hoard, Brayford House, Lucy Tower Street, Lincoln, LN1 1XN. First prize: £500. Judge: Mimi Khalvati.

Little Pub Co. Poetry Prize — PO Box 111, Kidderminster, Worcs DY14 9DZ. First prize: £1000. Special entry qualification "Entrants, who must be eighteen or over, must give an undertaking that they have consumed at least three pints of ale or its equivalent before writing a poem on the subject of 'drink', 'pubs' or 'experiences relating to drink'." Judge: Colm O'Rourke.

National Schizophrenia National Poetry Competition — 22 Rowland Road, Stevenage, Herts, SG1 11E. First prize: £100. Judge: Frances Wilson.

Newcastle Brown Ale Poetry Competition — c/o The Poetry Society, 22 Betterton Street, London, WC2H 9BU. First prize: £1000.

Norwich Writers' Circle Open Poetry Competition — 215 Wroxham Road, Norwich, NR7 8AQ. First prize: £100. Judge: Peter Scupham.

Nottingham Breast Cancer Trust Refurbishment Fund Open Poetry Competition — Margaret Pietryka, 64 Grangewood Road, Wollaton, Nottingham, NG8 2SW. First prize: Publication in *Poetry Nottingham* and tape of poem read by actress Jill Pearson. Judge: Terence Young.

Nottingham Poetry Society Open Competition — Aubrey Bush, 21 Fylingdale Way, Wallaton, Nottingham, NG8 2TH. First prize: £200. Judge: David Duncombe.

One Voice Monologue Competition — Theatr Cwmtawe, Parc Ynys-derw, Pontardawe, SA8 4BG. Judges: Simon Callow, Dwynwen Berry, Roger Fox, Kate Harwood. Prizes include Canon Star-writers plus professional performance.

Open University Poets Open Poetry Competition — Al Campbell, The Observatory, Cyncoed Gardens, Cardiff, CF2 6BH. First prize: £200. Judge: Peter Finch.

Orbis Rhyme International Competition — 199 The Long Shoot, Nuneaton, Warks, CV11 6JQ. First prize: £200. Judge: Alan Brownjohn.

Ouse Valley Poetry — 11 Woodville Ave, Crosby, Merseyside, L23 3BX. First prize: possibly £500. Judges: Leading poets.

Pen & Keyboard Autumn Writing Competition — SQR (Publishing) Enterprize, 526 Fulham Palace Road, London, SW6 6JE. First prize: £100. Judge: David Stern.

Peterloo Poets Open Poetry Competition — 2 Kelly Gardens, Calstock, Cornwall, PL18 9SA. First prize: £2000. Judges: Dannie Abse, Jackie Kay, Susan Roberts, Harry Chambers.

PHRAS Open Poetry Competition — 23 Jedburgh Street, London SW11 5QA. First prize: £150. Judges: Johnathon Clifford, Helen Robinson.

Poetry Business Competition — 51 Byram Arcade, Westgate, Huddersfield, HD1 1ND. Two joint winners published by Smith/Doorstop. Judge: Maura Dooley.

Poetry Digest Bard Of The Year — Alan Forrest, 28 Stainsdale Green, Whitwick, Leics, LE67 5PW. First prize: 1000 guineas. Judge: Dannie Abse.

Poetry Life Open Poetry Competition — 14 Remmington Oval, Lymington, Hants, SO41 8BQ. First prize: £200. Judge: *Poetry Life* magazine editors.

Poetry Society National Competition — 22 Betterton Street, London, WC2H 9BU. First prize: £3000. Judges: Helen Dunmore, Sean O'Brien, Anthony Thwaite.

Quartos Open Writing Competition — BCM-Writer, London, WC1N 3XX. First prize: £50. Judges: *Quartos* magazine editors.

Redbeck Press Poetry Competition — 24 Aireville Road, Frizinghall, Bradford BD9 5HH. First prize: book publication. Judge: David Tipton.

Richard Burton Poetry Competition — 74 Wildbrook, Taibach, Port Talbot, West Glamorgan, SA13 2UN. For spoken poetry. First prize: £200. Judges: Sally Roberts Jones, Alan Davies.

Ripley Poetry Association Open Competition — Alison Bennett, 42 Pembroke Road, Bromley, Kent, BR1 2RU. First prize: £250. Judge: George Szirtes.

Royal British Legion Poetry Competition — Mr A.R. Chadwick, 7 Stonebridge Road, Nantwich, Cheshire, CW5 7AY. First prize: £100. Judge: Laurence Cotterell.

Salisbury Open Poetry Competition — Alan White, 86 Norfolk Road, Salisbury, Wilts, SP2 8HG. First prize: £100. Judge: Roland John.

Salopian Poetry Society Open Competition — Lilian Parker, 54 Coronation Drive, Donnington, Telford, Shrops, TF2 8HY. First prize: £30.

Sheffield Thursday Creative Writing Competition — Sheffield Hallam University, School of Cultural Studies, 36 Collegiate Cres., Sheffield, S10 2BP. First prize: £1000. Judges: Barry Hines, Mimi Khalvati, E.A. Markham, Margaret Drabble.

Skoob International Poetry Competition — 15 Sicilian Avenue, Southampton Row, Holborn, London, WC1A 2QH. First prize: £1000 *Skoob* book token. Judges: Ruth Fainlight, Ted Hughes, Lucien Jenkins, Alan Ross.

Southport Writers' Circle Poetry Competition — A. Chisholm, 53 Richmond Road, Birkdale, Southport, Merseyside, PR8 4SB. First prize: £100. Judge: Roger Elkin.

South West Poetry Competition — Field Cottage, Trevissome, Flushing, Falmouth, TR11 5TA. First prize: £500.

Staple Open Poetry Competition — Tor Cottage, 81 Cavendish Road, Matlock, Derbys, DE4 3HD. First prize: £250. Judge: Fleur Adcock.

Suffolk Poetry Society Crabbe Memorial Poetry Competition — Mary Usherwood, 3283 Belstead Rd, Ipswich, Suffolk, 1P2 9EH. Entrants from Suffolk only. First prize: £100. Judges: Andrew Motion, Anthony Thwaite.

Sunk Island Publishing Open Poetry Competition — PO Box 74, Lincoln, LN1 1QC. First prize: £500. Judge: Catherine Byron.

Surrey Poetry Centre (Guildford & Wey Poets) Open Competition — Godfrey Heaven, 48 Woodlands Avenue, West Byfleet, Surrey, KT14 6AW. First prize: £150. Judge: Pauline Stainer.

Sussex Writers Club National Poetry Competition - 11a Beehive Lane, Ferring, West Sussex, BN12 5NN. First prize: £150. Judge: Fleur Adcock.

SWWJ Centenary Competition — Society of Women Writers and Journalists, Chris McCallum, PO Box 96, Altrincham, Cheshire, WA14 2LN. First prize: £150. Judge: Dannie Abse.

Swanage Arts Festival Literary Competition — Joy Martin, 42 Benlease Way, Swanage, Dorset, BH19 2SZ. First prize: £150. Judge: Owen Davis.

Table Magazine Poetry Competition — 11 Oulton Close, Aylesbury, Bucks, HP21 7JY. First prize: £50. Judge: Pauline Stainer.

Tees Valley Writer Story and Poetry Competition — 57 The Avenue, Linthorpe, Middlesbrough, TS5 6QU. First prize: £200.

Understanding Poetry Competition — 20a Montgomery Street, Edinburgh, EH7 5JS. First prize: £120.

Ver Poets Open Competition — 6 Chiswell Green Lane, St Albans, Herts, AL2 3AL. First prize: £500. Judge: Roland John.

Wells Festival of Literature Open Poetry Competition — 5 Market Place, Wells, Somerset, BA5 2RF. First prize: £100. Judge: Roland John.

West Sussex Writers' Club National Poetry Competition — Lady Smedley, 11a Beehive Lane, Ferring, West Sussex, BN12 5NN. First prize: £150. Judges: Fleur Adcock, Nicholas Fisk.

West Wales Writers' Umbrella Open Competition — Eurwen Price, Y Garn, Swansea Road, Llewitha, Fforestfach, Swansea, West Glamorgan, SA5 4NR. First prize: £50.

Woodman Press Poetry Competition — Jay Woodman, 14 Hillfield, Selby, North Yorkshire, Y08 OND. First prize: £75. Judge: Jay Woodman.

Wrekin Writers' Group Annual Open Poetry Competition — Peter Thomas, Haydock, New Works Lane, Little Wenlock, Telford, TF6 5BS. First prize: £25.

Writers Bureau Poetry Competion — 7 Dale Street, Manchester, M1 1JB. First prize: £200. Judge: Allison Chilsholm.

X.E. Nathan Open Poetry Award — PO Box 392, Cardiff, South Glamorgan, CF5 6YE. First prize: £1500. Judges: Roland John, Michael Schmidt.

Yorkshire Open Poetry Competition — Ilkley Literature Festival, 9a Leeds Road, Ilkley, West Yorkshire, LS29 8DH. First prize: £250. Judge: Liz Lochhead.

APPENDIX IV
Writers' Groups Meeting In Wales

Groups meet in a variety of venues ranging from private houses to public libraries. As described in Chapter Four most provide openings for poets. Details of meeting places and times are best checked before turning out.

North Wales

Chester Poets meet monthly. Secretary: Shelia Parry, 92 Glyn Garth, Blacon, Chester, CH1 5RZ.

Colwyn Writers' Circle meet every second Wednesday at the secretary's address at 2.30pm and every fourth Wednesday at Colwyn Bay Library at 7.30pm. Secretary: Mrs Eva Betts, Woodside, Pen Y Bryn Road, Upper Colwyn Bay, Clwyd, LL29 6AL.

Deeside Writers Group. Secretary: Chris Stork, 7 Vale Close, Broughton, CH1 OTA.

Conwy Valley Writers meet at Bradford House, Denbigh Street, Llanwrwst, Gwynedd, LL26 0BR. Secretary: Liz James, Bryn Eglwys, Penmachno, Gwynedd, LL24 0TY.

*I*D Books* meet every third Friday at Connah's Quay Library, other Fridays at Deeside Community Wing. Details from Connah's Quay Library. Tel: 0244 830485.

Holywell Literary Society meet monthly at 7.30pm every third Thursday at Victoria Hotel, High Street, Holywell. Secretary: Tecwyn Lloyd, 20 Plas Dewi, Well Street, Holywell, Clwyd, CH8 7PP. Tel: Holywell 715128.

Mold Writers meet on the first and third Monday of each month at Glanrafon Arts Centre. Details on 0352 754063.

Newtown Writers Group. Secretary: Chris Kinsey, 3 Cymberhill, The Fron, Newtown, Powys.

Prestatyn Writers meet fortnightly on Mondays at 7.30pm at the Grange Hotel near Suncentre. Secretary: Huw Jenkins, Englyn, Maes Derwen, St Asaph, Clwyd, LL17 0DA.

Rhosneigr Writers Group. Secretary Fiona C. Owen, Post Office Flat, Rhosneigr, Anglesey, Gwynedd, LL64 5JX.

Rhuthin Writers meet every Tuesday, 7.30pm, at the English Presbyterian Church, Wynnstay Road, Rhuthin. Secretary: Beverley Tinson, 100 Mwrog Street, Rhuthin. Tel: 0824 222944.

Rhyl Writers Group. Secretary: Claire Cider, 99 Ffordd Isa, Prestatyn, Clwyd.

Sword And Acorn Writers meet in Colwyn Bay. Secretary: Mr S.H. Aball, 363 Abergele Road, Old Colwyn, Colwyn Bay, Clwyd, LL29 9TL.

Wrexham Writers meet fortnightly at Wrexham Library and Arts Centre. Secretary: Pam Goodwin, Almere Farm, Rossett, Wrexham.

South Wales — Cardiff Area

Bulldog Writers meet Wednesdays at 10.00 am at the Bulldog Inn, Fairwater, Cardiff. Secretary: Pat Mansfield, 13 Quarry Cres, Cardiff. Tel: 0222 564122.

Cardiff Women Writers, Deadlier Than The Male, classes, performance evenings. Contact Gill Brightmore, 75 Fidlas Road, Cardiff. Tel: 0222 762267.

Cardiff Writers' Circle meet Mondays at 7.00pm, 61 Park Place, Cardiff. Secretary: Sybil Josty, 36 St Cadoc Road, Cardiff. Tel: 0222 623061.

Creative Writing Discoveries meet Monday at 7.00pm term time. A WEA course run by Liz Bletsoe at St Cyres Comprehensive School in Penarth. £1.50 per evening.

Adventures In Creative Writing. Term time classes tutored by Chris Torrance for the Cardiff University Extra Mural Department. Thursdays at 7.00pm term time. Contact 0222 874831/2 for more information.

Undercover Writers meet Tuesdays at 8.30pm, Four Bars Inn, Cardiff. Secretary: Christopher Mills, 122 Clive Street, Grangetown, Cardiff, CF1 7JE. Tel: 0222 231696.

Tŷ Celyn Writers meet Tuesdays at 7.00pm, Cardiff High School. Secretary: Kath Willison, 10 Ogwen Drive, Lakeside, Cardiff, CF2 6LH. Tel: 0222 755241.

Nightwriters meet Tuesdays at 7.00pm, Mackintosh Institute, Roath, Cardiff. Secretary: Thelma Harding. Tel: 0222 464558.

Dinas Powys Writers meet Wednesdays at 10.00 am. Secretary:

Rowland Powell, 14 Berkley Drive, Penarth, Cardiff. Tel: 0222 709702.

Penarth Writers meet Thursdays at 7.30pm at The Baptist Lounge, Stanwell Road, Penarth. Secretary: Mary Hughes, 40 Castle Drive, Dinas Powys, Cardiff. Tel: 0222 515147.

Rhiwbina Writers meet Mondays at 10.00am at Bethany Baptist Church. Secretary: Joan Hughes, 26 Thornbury Close, Cardiff, CF4 1UT. Tel: 0222 691020.

Taking Off: Women's Writing Group meet 6.00pm on Wednesdays during term time at Cardiff Central Library. Details from Jackie Aplin on 0222 451714.

South East Wales

Aberfan and Merthyr Vale Writers and History Group meet monthly. Contact Maureen Hughes, 44 Aberfan Road, Aberfan, CF48 4QL. Tel: 0443 690551.

Cynon Valley Writers meet Tuesdays at 7.00pm at The White Lion, Aberdare. Secretary: Wendy McGrath, 36 Albert Street, Aberdare, Mid-Glam. Tel: 0685 879773.

Bridgend Writers meet on the second Friday of each month at the Police Club, 7.30pm. Secretary: Mrs Munitich, 56 Hunters Ridge, Brackla, Bridgend. Tel: 0656 660514.

Merthyr Writers meet Fridays at 2.30pm at The Crown Inn, Merthyr. Secretary: Dorothy Craig, 1 Amberton Place, Penydarren, Methyr Tydfil. Tel: 0685 83050.

Noumena meet Tuesdays at 7.00pm at Clwb y Bont, Pontypridd. Secretary: John Evans, 9 Lanelay Terrace, Maesycoed, Pontypridd, CF37 1ER. Tel: 0443 403689.

University of Glamorgan Creative Writers meets at the Treforest campus during term time with tutor Helen Dunmore. Open to non-students. Contact Tony Curtis on 0443 482551.

Bedwas Writers' Group meet Mondays at 7.00pm at Bedwas Centre. Secretary: Sally Williams, 9 Tydfil Rd, Bedwas, Mid Glamorgan. Tel: 0222 888297.

Rhondda Writers meet on the first Friday of each month at Ton Pentre WMH, 7.30pm. Secretary: Cheryl Hier, 4 Ramah Street, Treorchy, Mid Glamorgan. Tel: 0443 772015.

Porthcawl Writers meet on the third Monday of each month at 24 Victoria Avenue, Porthcawl Secretary: Dilys M. Burge, 16 Sker

Walk, Porthcawl, CF36 3RA.

The Valleys Literature Group organise regular poems and pints evenings, days schools and other special events in the South Wales Valley areas. Contact Secretary Bob Mole on 0633 875075.

South East Wales — Gwent

Torfaen Writers meet Tuesday mornings at Trosnant House, Pontypool. Secretary: Roy Evans, 76 Fields Park Road, Newport. Tel: 0633 223554.

Creative Writers meet Tuesdays at 10.00am at Ashley House, Cwmbran. Contact Anne Cluysenaar on Usk 673797.

Risca Writers. Contact Sean O'Connell at 33 Snowdon Close, Risca, Gwent. Tel: 0633 613633.

Stow Hill Poets. Contact Joe Pumford at 65 Sycamore Avenue, Newport, Gwent. Tel: 0633 282235.

Islwyn Writers meet Tuesday at 2.30pm at Blackwood Library. Secretary: Roger Williams, 50 Redland Street, Newport, Gwent NP9 5L2. Tel: 0633 853170.

Gwent Poetry Society meet monthly at the Dolmen Theatre, Newport. Secretary: Ms L. Davies, 21 Worcester Cr., Newport, Gwent, NP9 7NX. Tel: 0633 256444.

Newport Writers meet Mondays at 7.30pm, Brynglas House, Newport. Secretary: Ann Tripp, 9 Bettws Close, Newport, Gwent NP9 5HG. Tel: 0633 852094.

Abertillery Writers meet Mondays at 7.00pm, Coach and Horses, Six Bells. Secretary: D. Meacham, 131 King St., Cwm, Ebbw Vale, Gwent, NP3 6SJ. Tel: 0495 309597.

Monmouth Writers meet Thursdays at 7.00pm, Three Horseshoes. Secretary: Maxine Williams, 32 Kings Fee, Monmouth, Gwent, NP5 3BW. Tel: 0600 714723.

Tredegar Writers meet Saturdays at 2.00pm, Tredegar Library. Secretary: Michael Davies, 58 Kimberley Terrace, Tredegar, Gwent, NP2 3LD. Tel: 0495 255335.

Cwmbran Writers meet on alternate Fridays and Saturdays at Cwmbran Library. Secretary: Betty Hayward, 9 Eridge Road, Garndiffaith, Pontypool, NP4 7LU. Tel: 0495 774706.

The Collective meet twice monthly at The Hill in Abergavenny. Contact secretary John Jones on 0873 856350.

Potty Poets and Wicked Writers for children at Abersychan Library. Contact Secretary Lorna Lloyd, Brynmern, Old Lane, Abersychan, Pontypool, Gwent, NP4 7DQ. Tel: 0495 774867.

Blackwood Young Writers meet every Monday at Blackwood M.I., 5.45 - 7.30pm. Secretary: Patrick Jones, 5 Criccieth Close, Grove Park, Blackwood. Tel: 0495 222150.

Abergavenny Bookworms. Contact Anita Saunders, 22 Greystones Cres., Abergavenny, NP7 6JY. Tel: 0873 855221.

Pontypool District Writers meet Monday afternoons at Abersychan Library. Secretary: Ken Clark, 1 Varteg Rd, Varteg, Pontypool, Gwent. Tel: 0495 773073.

South East Wales — Elsewhere

Hay-on-Wye Writers. Contact Mrs A. Edmondes, Upper Dulas, Cusop Dingle, Hay-on-Wye, HR3 6HW. Tel: 0497 820798.

Mid-Border Community Arts at the Shire Hall, Presteigne, LD8 2AD hold regular writers' meetings. Contact Joan Rees on 0544 267276.

South & Mid Wales Association of Writers (SAMWAW) run regular conferences, writers' weekends, and other meetings and performances in the South Wales area. Contact Julian Rosser, c/o IMC Consulting Group, Denham House, Lambourne Cres, Cardiff, CF4 5ZW. Tel: 0222 761170.

South West Wales

Manselton Writers' Group. Contact Don Allen, 354 Pentregethin Road, Gendros, Swansea, SA5 8AJ.

Fishguard Writers' Group. Contact C.A. Byrne-Sutton, Ingli Cottage, Bryn Henllan, Dinas Cross, Pembs, SA42 0SD.

Coronation School Writers. Contact Veronica Huntley, Kelmscott, Reynalton Kilgetty, South Pembs, SA68 OPH.

Neath Writers. Contact Neal Mason, 17 Brynawel, Pontardawe SA8 4JP.

Afan Poetry Society meets every second Monday of the month at Afan Arts Centre, Port Talbot. Contact Norman Jones, 74 Wildbrook, Taibach, Port Talbot, West Glamorgan.

Pontardawe Writers Group meets every other Thursday at 6.45pm in the Cross Centre, Pontardawe. Contact Bella Mills, Glan yr

Onnen, Gurnos Road, Ystradgynlais, Swansea, West Glamorgan, SA9 2JY.

Swansea Writing Workshop. Contact Rita Wilkinson, 22 Bishopston Road, Bishopston, Swansea, West Glamorgan.

Swansea Writers' Circle. Contact Beth Quinn, 932 Carmarthen Road, Fforestfach, Swansea, West Glamorgan.

Swansea Arts Magazine Poetry Reading every Friday during term time at the North Arts Coffee Bar, University of Swansea, Singleton Park, Swansea.

Gorseinon Poetry Initiative. Enquiries to David Thomas, 93 High St, Gorseinon, SA4 4BL. Tel: 0792 893107.

Penlan Poets and Writers Group meet every other Wednesday at the Community Centre, Heol Frank, Penlan, Swansea. Tel: 0792 587620.

Carmarthen Writers' Circle. Contact Madeline Mayne, 79 Bronwydd Road, Carmarthen, Dyfed, SA31 2AP.

Lampeter Writers' Workshop. Contact Sue Moules, 44 Maesyderi, Lampeter, Dyfed, SA48 7EP.

Circle of Writers Aberystwyth And Area. Contact Sybil King, Glenona, Abermad, Llanfarian, Aberystwyth, Dyfed, SY23 4ET.

Llanelli Writers' Circle meets the last Wednesday of the month at 2.00pm in Llanelli Children's Library. Contact Carole A. Smith, 20 Rectory Close, Loughor, West Glamorgan, SA4 2JU.

Pembroke Dock Writers' Circle, contact Ken Morgan, 66 Heywood Crescent, Tenby, Dyfed. Groups meet both mornings and evenings.

Pembrokeshire Writers' Circle, contact Jeremy Streets, 12 James Street, Neyland, Dyfed.

Teifi Writers' Circle, contact Daphne White, Graig Farm, Llangynog, Carmarthen, Dyfed.

Port Talbot Writers' Group meet fortnightly at Afan Arts Centre. Contact Haydn Harries, 10 Kenilworth Court, Baglan, Port Talbot, West Glamorgan. Tel: 0639 814759.

Neath Writers' Group meet every Friday at 2.00pm in Neath Town Library, Victoria Gardens. Contact Chris Stephens, 26 Harle Street, Neath, West Glamorgan. Tel: 0639 637498. An evening group meets every Thursday, 7.00pm. Contact Paul Lewis, tel: 0639 630096.

Tywi Valley and District Writers' Circle. Contact Secretary C.P. Jones. Tel: 0558 823845.

APPENDIX IV

More information on new groups can be found by contacting your local library who can also provide information on creative writing day and evening classes running in their areas.

Appendix V
Poetry Small Mags: Addresses

The following list covers some of the main little magazine outlets for poetry in the UK. It is by no means complete and poets intending to submit material are advised to buy a copy of the periodical concerned before sending in. Details of further magazines will be found in the directories listed in Chapter One. Details of magazines based in Wales will also be found at the end of that Chapter.

Active In Airtime, Ralph Hawkins & others, 53 East Hill, Colchester, CO1 2QY.

Acumen, Patricia Oxley, 6 The Mount, Higher Furzeham, Brixham, Devon, TQ5 8QY.

Agenda, 5 Cranbourne Court, Albert Bridge Road, London, SW11 4PE.

Ambit, Martin Bax, 17 Priory Gardens, Highgate, London, N6 5QY.

And, 89a Petherton Rd, London, N5 2QT.

Angel Exhaust, Andrew Duncan, Flat 6, Avon Court, Holden Rd, London, N12 8HR.

Aquarius, Eddie Lindon, Flat 3, 116 Sutherland Avenue, London, W9.

Bête Noir, John Osbourne, American Studies Dept., The University, Cottingham Road, Hull, HU6 7RX.

Blithe Spirit, Journal of the British Haiku Society, 27 Park Street, Westcliff-on-sea, Essex, BS0 7PA.

Blue Cage, 98 Bedord Road, Birkdale, Southport, Merseyside, PR8 4HL.

Bogg, George Cairncross, 31 Belle Vue Street, Filey, North Yorkshire.

The Bound Spiral, M. Petrucci, 72 First Avenue, Bush Hill Park, Enfield, Middx, EN1 1BW.

Braquemanrd, David Allenby, 20 Terry Street, Hull, HU3 1UD.

Brimstone, Isabel Gillard, St Laurence Cottage, Sellman Street, Gnosall, Stafford, ST20 0EP.

Candelabrum, M.L.McCarthy, 9 Milner Road, Wisbech, Cambridgeshire, PE13 2LR.

Chapman, 4 Broughton Place, Edinburgh, EH1 3RX.

Dial 174, 8 Higham Green, King's Lynn, Norfolk, PE30 4RX.

Doors, 61 West Borough, Wimbourne, Dorset, BH21 1LX.

Dog, 32b Breakspears Road, London, SE4 1UW.

The Echo Room, Brendan Cleary, 45 Bewick Court, Princess Square, Newcastle-upon-Tyne, NE1 8HG.

Edinburgh Review, Peter Kravitz, Edinburgh University Press, 22 George Square, Edinburgh, EH8 9LF.

Envoi, 44 Rudyard Road, Biddulph Moor, Stoke on Trent, ST8 7JN.

Exile, John Herbert Marr, 38 Emerald Street, Saltburn, TS12 1ED.

Fat Chance, Louise Hudson & Mary Maher, Lake Cottage, South Street, Sheepwash, Beaworthy, Devon.

First Offence, Syringa, The Street, Stodmarsh, Canterbury, CT3 4BA.

First Time, Josephine Austin, 4 Burdett Place, George Street, Hastings, TN34 3ED.

Foolscap, 78 Friars Road, East Ham, London, E6 1LL.

Fragmente, 8 Hertford Street, Oxford, OX4 3AJ.

The Frogmore Papers, 42 Morehall Avenue, Folkestone, Kent, CT19 4EF.

Gairfish, W.N.Herbert, 34 Gillies Place, Dundee, DO5 3LE.

Global Tapestry Journal, Dave Cunliffe, Spring Bank, Longsight Rd, Copster Green, Blackburn, Lancs, BB1 9EU.

Granite, Alan M. Kent, Southview, Wheal Bull, Foxhole, St Austell, Cornwall, PL26 7UA.

Grille, Simon Smith, 53 Ormonde Court, Upper Richmond Rd, Putney, London, SW15 5TP.

Haiku Quarterly, Kevin Bailey, 39 Exmouth Street, Swindon, Wilts, SN1 3PU.

Heart Throb, Mike Parker, 95 Spencer St, Birmingham, B18 6DA.

The Honest Ulsterman, Tom Clyde, 14 Shaw St, Belfast, BT4 1PT.

Iota, 67 Hady Cres., Chesterfield, Derbys, S41 0EB.

Iron, Peter Mortimer, 5 Marden Tce., Cullercoats, North Shields, Tyne and Wear, NE30 4PD.

Issue One/The Bridge, Ian Brocklebank, 2 Tewkesbury Drive, Grimsby, South Humberside.

Krax, 63 Dixon Lane, Leeds, LS12 4RR.

Kroklok, Bob Cobbing, 89a Petherton Road, London, N5 2QT.

Lallans (Lowlands Scots), David Purves, 8 Strathalmond Road, Edinburgh, EH4 8AD.

Lines Review, MacDonald publishers, Edgefield Road, Loanhead, Midlothian, EH20 9SY.

London Magazine, 30 Thurloe Place, London, SW7.

Memes, Norman Jope, 28 Molesworth Road, Plympton, Plymouth, Devon.

Never Bury Poetry, Bettina Jones, 30 Beryl Ave., Tottington, Bury, Lancs, BL8 3NF.

New Departures, Mike Horovitz, Piedmont, Bisley, Stroud, Glos, GL6 7BU.

New Hope International, Gerald England, 20 Werneth Avenue, Gee Cross, Hyde, Cheshire, SK14 5NL.

Nineties Poetry, 33 Landsdowne Place, Hove, BN3 1HF.

The North, 51 Byram Arcade, Westgate, Huddersfield, HD1 1ND.

Northwords, Angus Dunn, West End Cottage, Blairninich, Strathpeffer, Rossshire.

Northlight, 136 Byres Rd, Glasgow, G12 8TD.

Oasis, 12 Stevenage Road, London, SW6 6ES.

Object Permanence, 121 Menock Road, Kingspark, Glasgow, G44 5SD.

Odyssey, Derrick Woolf, Coleridge Cottage, Nether Stowey, Somerset.

Orbis, 199 The Long Shoot, Nuneaton, Warwickshire, CV11 6JQ.

Ore, 7 The Towers, Stevenage, Herts, SG1 1HE.

Ostinato, The Tenormen Press, PO Box 522, London, N8 7SZ.

Otter, Mark Beeson & others, Little Byspock, Richmond Rd, Exeter, Devon.

Outposts, Roland John, 22 Whitewell Road, Frome, Somerset BA11 4EL.

Oxford Poetry, Sinead Garrigan & Kate Reeves, Magdalen College, Oxford, OX1 4AU.

Pages, Robert Sheppard, 239 Lessingham Ave, London, SW17 8NQ.

Parataxis, Drew Milne, School of English Studies, Arts Building, University of Sussex, Falmer, Brighton, BN1 9NA.

Passion, 18 Chaddesley Rd, Kidderminster, Worcs, DY10 3AD.

Pause, 27 Mill Road, Fareham, Hants, PO16 0TH.

Pennine Platform, Brian Merrikin Hill, Ingmanthorpe Hall Farm Cottage, Wetherby, West Yorks, LS22 5EQ.

The People's Poetry, P.G.P. Thompson, 71 Harow Cres., Romford, Essex, RM3 7BJ.

PN Review, 208 Corn Exchange, Manchester, M4 3BQ.

Poetry And Audience, School of English, University of Leeds, LS2 9JT.

Poetry Digest, Bradgate Press, 28 Stainsdale Green, Whitwick, Leicester, LE67 5PW.

Poetry Durham, M. O'Neill, Dept of English, University of Durham, Elvet Riverside, New Elvet, Durham, DH1 3JT.

Poetry Ireland Review, 44 Upper Mount Street, Dublin 2, Ireland.

Poetry Life, 14 Pennington Oval, Lymington, Hants, SO41 8BQ.

Poetry London Newsletter, Box 4LF, London, W1A 4LF.

Poetry Nottingham, Martin Holroyd, 39 Cavendish Road, Long Eaton, Nottingham, NG10 4HY.

Poetry Now, 1-2 Wainman Rd, Woodston, Peterborough, PE2 7BU.

Poetry Review, Peter Forbes, 22 Betterton Street, London, WC2H 9BU.

Poet's Voice, 12 Dartmouth Ave., Bath, BA2 1AT.

Pomes, 23 Bright Street, York YO2 4XS.

The Printer's Devil, Top offices, 13a Western Rd, Hove, East Sussex, BN3 1AE.

Psychopoetica, Geoff Lowe, Dept of Psychology, University of Hull, Hull, HU6 7RX.

Purple Patch, Geoff Stevens, 8 Beaconview House, Charlemont Farm Estate, West Bromwich, B71 3PL.

Quartos, BCM Writer, London, WC1N 3XX.

Ramraid Extra Ordinaire, Kerry Sowerby, 2 Midland Road, Leeds, LS6 1BQ.

Rhyme Arrival, 1-2 Wainman Rd, Woodston, Peterborough, PE2 7BU.

Rustic Rub, Jay Woodman, 14 Hillfield, Selby, N. Yorks, YO8 0ND.

The Rialto, 32 Grosvenor Road, Norwich, NR2 2PZ.

The Salmon, Auburn, Upper Fairhill, Galway, Eire.

Scratch, Mark Robinson, 9 Chestnut Road, Eaglescliffe, Stockton-on-Tees, TS16 0BA.

Sepia, Colin Webb, Knill Cross House, Nr Anderton Road, Millbrook, Torpoint, Cornwall, PL10 1DX.

Shearsman, 47 Dayton Close, Plymouth, Devon, PL6 5DX.

Smith's Knoll, Roy Blackman & Michael Laskey, 49 Church Road, Little Glemham, Woodbridge, Suffolk, IP13 0BJ.

Smoke, Dave Ward, Windows, 40 Canning Street, Liverpool, L8 7NP.

Stand, 179 Wingrove Road, Newcastle upon Tyne, NE4 9DA.

Staple, Don Measham & Bob Windsor, Tor Cottage, 81 Cavendish Road, Matlock, Derbyshire, DE4 3HD.

Southfields, 98 Gresenhall Rd, Southfields, London SW18 5QJ.

Spokes, 45 Clophill Rd, Upper Gravenshurst, Bedford MN45 4JH.

The Steeple, Three Spires Press, Killeen, Blackrock Village, Cork, Ireland.

Sunk Island Review, Michael Blackburn, PO Box 74, Lincoln, LN1 1QC.

Symphony, Bemerton Press, 9 Hamilton Gardens, London, NW8 9PU.

Tabla, PO Box 93, Lancaster, Lancs, LA1 3HB.

Tandem, 13 Stephenson Rd, Barbourne, Worcester, WR1 3EB.

Tears in the Fence, David Caddy, 38 Hod View, Stourpaine, Nr Blandford Forum, Dorset, DT11 8TN.

Tees Valley Writer, Derek Gregory, 57 The Avenue, Linthorpe, Middlesborough, Cleveland, TS5 6QU.

The Third Half, 16 Fane Close, Stamford, Lincs, PE9 1HG.

TOPS (incorporating *Cowpat*, *Canto* & *Toadbird*), Rose Cottage, 17 Hadassah Grove, Lark Lane, Liverpool, L17 8AX.

Uncompromising Positions, Cheryl Wilkinson, 92 Staneway, Leam Lane, Gateshead, Tyne & Wear, NE10 8LS.

Unicorn, 12 Milton Ave, Milbrook, Stalybridge, Cheshire, SK15 3HB.

Verse, Dept of English, The University, St Andrews, Fife, KY16 9AL.

Walking Naked, 13 Napier St, Swinton, Manchester, M27 3JQ.

West Coast Magazine, Unit 7, 29 Brand St, Glasgow, G51 1DN.

Westwords, Dave Woolley, 15 Trelawney Road, Peverell, Plymouth, PL3 4JS.

Weyfarers, Margaret Palin, Hilltop Cottage, 9 White Rose Lane, Woking, Surrey, GU22 7JA.

The Wide Skirt, Geoff Hattersley, 28 St Helens Street, Elsecar, Barnsley, South Yorks, S74 8BH.

Wits End, a magazine by new writers, 27 Pheasant Close, Winnersh, Wokingham, Berkshire, RG11 5LS.

Writing Women, 7 Cavendish Place, Newcastle upon Tyne, NE2 2NE.

Working Titles, 29 St Martin's Rd, Knowle, Bristol, B54 2NQ.

Words Worth, 1 Dairy Cottage, Compton Rd, South Cadbury, Yeovil, Somerset, BA22 7E2.

Appendix VI
Poetry Small Presses: Addresses

Small presses are usually more difficult to track than periodicals. Many have been set up only to publish their owners or the work of a small closed circle. Others publish a single title then vanish. Those listed here are known to have been active in recent times. Commercial publishers with an interest in poetry along with poetry specialists, as discussed in Chapter Eleven, have not been included. Details of presses based in Wales will be found in the list at the end of Chapter Five. Poets intending to submit mss are advised to write first, sending a stamped addressed envelope, and to consider sending material only where there has been a positive response. Listings here are by no means exhaustive and I have concentrated on those who publish a range of writers rather than the works of one poet. New presses are starting up all the time. Check out the directories detailed in Chapter One for further information.

Acumen Publications, 6 The Mount, High Furzeham, Brixham, South Devon, TQ5 8QY.
Agenda Editions, 5 Cranbourne Court, Albert Bridge Road, London SW11 4PE.
Allardyce, Barnett, 14 Mount Street, Lewes, East Sussex, BN7 1HL.
Aloes Books, Jim Pennington, 110 Mountview Road, London, N4 4JX.
Amazing Collosal Press, Maureen Richardson, 4 Gretton Road, Mapperley, Nottingham, NG3 5JT.
Arrival Press, (including *Poetry Now, Anchor Books, Forward Press*) 2-3 Wulfric Square, Peterborough, PE3 8RF.
Autolycus Press, 15 Barlby Rd, London ,W10 6AR.
Big Little Poem Books, 3 Park Avenue, Melton Mowbray, Leicestershire, LE13 0JB.
Black Cygnet Press, 33 Hastings Ave, Merry Oaks, Durham, DH1 3QC.
Blackstaff Press, 3 Galway Park, Dundonald, BT16 0AN.
Brentham Press, Margaret Tims, 40 Oswald Road, St Albans, Herts.
Carnivorus Arpeggio, 329 Beverley Road, Hull, HU5 1LD.
Crescent Moon, 18 Chadderley Rd, Kidderminster, Worcs, DY10 3AD.
Creation Press, 83 Clerkenwell Road, London, EC1M 5RJ.

Dangaroo Press, PO Box 20, Hebden Bridge, West Yorks, HX7 502.

Dedalus Poetry Press, 24 The Heath, Cypress Downs, Dublin 6, Ireland.

Diamond Press, 5 Berners Mansions, 34 Berners Street, London, W1P 3DA.

Dog and Bone, 175 Queen Victoria Drive, Scotstown, Glasgow, G12 9BP.

Dragonheart Press, 11 Mennin Road, Allestree, Derby, DE22 2NL.

Flambard Press, Peter Elfed Lewis, 4 Mitchell Avenue, Jesmond, Newcastle-Upon-Tyne, NEL 3LA.

Forest Books, Brenda Walker, 20 Forest View, Chingford, London, E4 7AY.

Forward Press, 1-2 Wainman Road, Woodston, Peterborough, PE2 7BJ.

Gallery Press, Peter Fallon, Loughcrew, Oldcastle, County Meath, Ireland.

Galloping Dog Press, 29 Hartside Gdns, Newscastle Upon Tyne, NE2 2JR.

Greville Press, Emscote Lawn, Astborn, Warwick, CV34 5QD.

Hangman Books, 2 May Rd, Rochester, Kent, ME1 2HY.

Headland Publications, Gladys Mary Coles, 38 York Avenue, West Kirby, Merseyside, L48 3LF.

Hearing Eye Press, John Rety, Box 1, 99 Tomano Avenue, London, NW5.

Hippopotamus Press, Roland John, 22 Whitewell Road, Frome, Somerset, BA11 4EL.

Iron Press, Peter Mortimer, 5 Marden Terrace, Cullercoats, North Shields, Tyne and Wear, NE30 4PD.

Jackson's Arm, Michael Blackburn, Box 74, Lincoln, LN1 1QC.

Jugglers Fingers Press, Cheryl Wilkinson, 92 Staneway, Leam Lane, Gateshead, Tyne & Wear, NE10 8LS.

Katabasis, Dinah Livingstone, 10 St Martin's Close, London, NW1 OHR.

KQBX Press, James Sale, 16 Scotter Road, Poverstown, Bournemouth, BH7 6LY.

KT Publications, 16 Fane Close, Stamford, Lincs, PE9 1HG.

Lymes Press, Greenfields , Agger Hill, Finney Green, Newcastle under Lyme, Staffs, ST5 6AA.

Making Waves Press, PO Box 226, Guildford, Surrey, GU3 1EW.

Mammon Press (UK contact for *University of Salzburg Press*), Fred Beake, 12 Dartmouth Avenue, Bath, BA2 1AT.

Many Press, 15 Norcott Road, London, N16 7BJ.

Mariscat Press, 3 Mariscat Road, Glasgow, G41 4ND.

National Poetry Foundation, 27 Mill Road, Fareham, Hants, PO16 0TH.

North and South, 23 Egerton Road, Twickenham, Middx, TW2 7SL.

Odyssey Poets, Coleridge Cottage, Nether Stowey, Somerset, TA5 1NQ.

Other Press, 19b Marriott Road, London, N4 3QN.

Pickpockets, 25 St Marn's Terrace, Hastings, East Sussex, TN34 3LS.

Pig Press, 7 Cross View Tce, Durham, DH1 4JY.

Poetical Histories, 27 Sturton Street, Cambridge, CB1 2QC.

The Poetry Business, Smith/Doorstop, 51 Byram Arcade, Westgate, Huddersfield, West Yorks, HO1 1ND.

Prest Roots Press, 34 Alpine Court, Lower Ladyes Hill, Kenilworth, CV8 2GP.

Ram Press, 42 Bradmore Park Rd, London, N6 0DT.

Reality Street Editions, 4 Howard Court, Peckham Rye, London, SE15 3PH.

Redbeck Press, David Tipton, 24 Aireville Road, Frizinghall, Bradford, BD9 4HH.

Rockingham Press, 11 Musley Lane, Ware, Herts, SG12 7EN.

Satis, Knoll Hill house, Ampleforth, West End, York, Y06 4DU.

Scratch Publications, 9 Chestnut Road, Englescliffe, Stockton-on-Tees, TS16 0BA.

Shearsman Books, 47 Dayton Close, Plymouth, PL6 5DX.

Skoob Books, 25 Lowman Road, London, N7 6DD.

Slow Dancer Press, Flat 2, 59 Parliament Hill, London, NW3 2TB.

Spectacular Diseases, 83b London Road, Peterborough, Cambs, PE2 9BS.

Staple First Editions, Tor Cottage, 81 Cavendish Road, Matlock, Derbyshire, DE4 3HD.

Stride Publications, Taxus Press, 11 Sylvan Road, Exeter, Devon, EX4 6EW.

Taranis Books, 2 Hugh Miller Place, Edinburgh, EH3 5JG.

Tenormen Press, PO Box 522, London, N8 7SZ.

Tuba Press, Tunley Cottage, Tunley, Nr Cirencester, Glos, GL7 6LW.

Turret Books/Steam Press, Bernard Stones, 36 Great Queen Street, London, WC2B 5AA.

A Twist In The Tail, Paul Cookson, PO Box 25, Refford, Notts, DN22 7ER.

Ulsterman Pamphlets, 14 Shaw St, Belfast, BT4 1PT.

Vennel Press, 9 Pankhurst Court, Caradon Close, London, E11 4TB.

Wellsweep Press, 1 Grove End House, 150 Highgate Road, London, NW5 1PD.

Writers Forum, Bob Cobbing, 89a Petherton Road, London, N5 2QT.

Zum Zum Books, Goshem, Bunlight, Drumnadrochit, Inverness-shire.

The Author

Peter Finch was born in Cardiff where he still lives. He is a poet, short fiction writer, performer and literary entrepreneur. He made his amrk as a sound and experimental poet although these days works on a much broader range of fronts. He is the manager of the Arts Council of Wales's bookshop, Oriel. His poetry books include *Poems for Ghosts* (Seren), *Make* (Galloping Dog), *Selected Poems* (Poetry Wales Press) and *Five Hundred Cobbings* (Writers Forum), while his best sellers are *How To Publish Your Poetry* and *How To Publish Yourself* (both Allison and Busby).